C000144050

A Life

Through Faith

With Poetry

A selection of poems written over a
lifetime, capturing life's highs and lows,
often through the lens of Carol's faith.

Carol Pigford

ISBN: 9798736372584

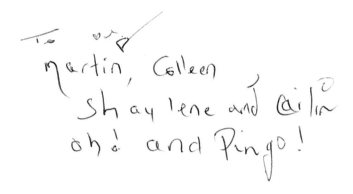

To our
Martin, Colleen
Shaylene and Cailin
oh! and Pingo!

DEDICATION

This book is dedicated to the many people who have given my Christian walk the value that it has.

You know who you are!

Last but not least, my own three precious sons and my four gorgeous grandchildren.

Who would have
believed this!
A book at age 74.
Rambling in my youth!
Love you all dear!
God Bless Mum xx

CONTENTS

Walking On Life's Way 11

Hurting...12

Hail, Magnified Jesus 14

Succour Me, Lord 15

Mischief and Play 16

Found In Me..18

Our Son Neil..19

Is It Enough? 22

God Is Seen..23

A Place for You..24

All I Ask, Dear Lord...26

Live for Jesus 27

Thoughts About You 28

Shadows...30

The Winter Tree...31

Degradation...34

Artificial Limb...35

Our Mum!..36

A Storm...38

Fearful 39

Desire for God 40

Breakdown 41

Teach Me, Jesus..44

The Future for Me 45

Valentine 46

A Prayer 47

My Feelings 48

I'm Free 49

Changes 50

His Name! 51

Rebellion 52

Dave and Jayne 53

Hospital Stay 54

Walking Ahead, Not in Fantasy 56

Questioning 57

Your Work and My Pain 58

Thank You for the Good Times 60

Sadness and Joy 61

Youth 62

My Dad 63

Grow 64

My Worry 66

Fill Me With Your Spirit, Lord 67

Trust 68

Remember Me 69

Why 70

Make Time for God's Kingdom 71

A Battle 72

Seasons...73

After Gethsemane..74

For Penny and Barbara 75

Stay By Me..76

Enduring..77

Anger...78

My Temple Must Not Be.....................................79

Life With God Shall Be.......................................80

Lessons...81

Am I a Fool?..82

May the Lord Bless You 83

Emotional Turmoil..84

Living for God...86

Poem of God..88

Crown Him and Hail Him...................................89

Worship 90

The Shadow of His Wings...................................91

Praise for the King...92

Praise 94

Mr Benjamin 95

Dear Sister...96

Climbing With Jesus 98

New Life Created 99

Walking Home... 100

A Pace of Life... 102

Looking Back 103

Easter 104

Standing Firm 106

Love of the Father 107

Launch Out 108

Let Me Burn Myself Away 109

A Witness for Jesus 110

A Flower 112

My Name Is In His Hands 113

Faith 114

Being Planted 116

Springs In Valleys 117

Today for That Day 118

Picking Fruit 119

A Tree 120

Teaching Me? 121

God's Care 122

Spring 124

Death's Sting 125

Pedestals of Pride 126

Physician's Balm 128

The Spirit at Work 129

Memories 130

Pain 131

Jonah 132

Deep and Dig.. 133

Sacred Tear... 134

Love.. 136

It Is Finished.. 137

Glory of the Lord... 138

A Song.. 140

Teach Me Thy Way.. 141

Caring.. 142

Narrow Way.. 143

Standing On Holy Ground....................................... 144

Always Seeing and Always Caring............................... 146

Friendship.. 147

Feeling Alone... 148

The Tears... 150

Happy Today 151

A Birth Journey 152

Am I Not a Christian?... 154

We Sing... 155

Heart of the Father... 156

A Friend's Wedding.. 158

Jealousy 159

The Sands of Time... 160

I Want to Be Free to Be Me.................................... 161

Three Precious Friends 162

Prayer and Trust.. 164

The Sabbath 165

Aspects of Autumn 166

Set Firm 168

Times of Need...169

Jimmy!...170

A Lark Is On the Wing...171

Gaze Upon Him 172

A Babe Is Born..173

Heart's Desire..174

True Friends 175

New Things 176

Heart and Soul...178

Trust Me...179

Jesus, I Feel Alone 180

Laughter...182

Dark and Bleak..183

At the Feet of Jesus 184

Ashes...186

The Redeemed Of the Lord 187

Cast All Self Out 188

Our Baby 190

Take Courage in the Lord 191

Be Still...192

Forgiveness 193

Leaving Friends..194

How Can I Bear the Anguish?.. 196

A Miscarriage 197

One Day 198

Doubting and Trusting... 200

Family.. 201

Mysterious Stranger 202

Short Poems and Expressions 203

In God's Everlasting Arms 206

WALKING ON LIFE'S WAY

As I've walked along life's way
I've prayed to God there would come a day
When He would supply my need
Of a friend true in word and deed.

I patiently looked here and there
But no one ever seemed to care.
When I was at the very end
God decided to give me that friend
That friend, yes, it is you!

I thank God for that wonderful day
When He led your path to mine
Your help and support in my time of need
Proved to me you are indeed
A friend with whom I'll walk
To life's end with Christ into Eternity.

HURTING

The pain, the agony and the despair
Lord, with me are You there?
This is hell.

Abba, Saviour and Comforter, three in one
I cling to You but remember, if I let go
You hold on.

Three in one, precious to me
How long the pain and agony?
Help me to bear the anguish and hurt
Heal my bruised and aching heart
I cry, Oh Lord, help me
The pain is tearing me apart.

Hold me, Jesus, in Your everlasting arms
Comfort me and bring my soul calm
Let me feel the gentle relief
That the precious Comforter brings.

My child, healing is flying to you on wings
Trust me now for each minute of the day
My love is great and I will not let you go
Be confident and safe because I tell you so.

I have brought you through suffering before
Believe that I will again bring you through this door
I can, my child, for my promises never fail
Test and trust believing in Me
Step out into faith
And I promise you will be kept safe
My arms are around you tight
Be still and I will give you light
Comfort and peace, joy and relief
Thank You, Jesus, I do believe
Oh, blessed release.

HAIL, MAGNIFIED JESUS

Hail, magnified Jesus
No longer crowned with thorns
Crowned with glory now!

Hail, magnified Jesus
No longer clothed in scarlet robe
Clothed in glory now!

Hail, magnified Jesus
We bow before Thee
With sincerity
Secure in Your authority
Now, no longer crucified
But magnified!

Hail, Jesus!
Our glorious King
Hail and praise Him
Jesus, our Lord and King!

SUCCOUR ME, LORD

Succour me, Lord, to Yourself
Drawing me to the fullness of Your love
Then the pain shall be borne
My heart, no longer torn.

Praise be to Jesus again
For lifting me out of the miry clay
And setting my feet on the King's highway
The hurts within my being are healing
Due to God's eye, all seeing.

He is touching, restoring and healing
Knowing just how I am feeling
So use me for Your glory
To tell all the wonderful story.

Loving and gracious is our King
Drawing us back again
Through our joys, sickness and pain
To fellowship with Him again.

MISCHIEF AND PLAY

I feel mischievous, I feel naughty
I feel like teasing and making laughter.

Will you laugh with me?
Will you run beneath the trees?
Will you hold me tight
When the time is right?

Will you swim with me
Splashing, shouting and sharing?
Will you lie with me
Loving, caressing and caring?

Will you laugh and play
Or will you run away?
Will you jump and shout for joy
As a child with a brand-new toy?
We shall have fun doing happy things!

Do you want to play with me?
Shall we play hide and seek?
I shall hide and you shall seek
Then you shall hide and I shall seek
But beware, once I've found you
I will never let you go
So don't say I never told you so!

Back to the beginning
Will you now play with me
Bouncing balls on our knees?
Making sandcastles or mud pies?
With you I know that I'm alive
Are you prepared to take the risk?
For the games I play are for keeps!
I dare you - chicken?
Okay, I will give you another chance
To come and play and hold my hand.

But if you play, it is for keeps
And I will never let you go
For, my friend, I need you so.

FOUND IN ME

Jesus, be found in me
Cleansing waters
Cleansing deep
Cleansing free.

Jesus, be found in me
Running waters
Running deep
Running free.

Jesus, be found in me
Living waters
Living deep
Living free.

In the core of my being
And in the heart of my heart.

Jesus, be found in me
Cleansing
Running
Living
Free in me.

OUR SON NEIL

Our son Neil
Is a flower in bud
Youthful and sparkling like the dew on the rose
Lord, as he gently unfolds his petals
Bring grace, life and love to his heart
Lord, don't ever let his petals split or part
Thank You, God, he is unfolding in Your heart.

As he gently unfolds before Your Son
Tender, strong and rich let him be
God, You only know what he means to me.

And Lord, as he grows strong roots in You
Help him to be true to himself and You
Keep those petals strong with rich love
And along life's way, let his fragrance rest and stay
With all those he meets.

Let him a blessing be
Solid growing in Thee
And as those petals stretch before Your Son
Lord and Father, make him one
With You, Mother Nature and his fellow man
As he walks along life's way
Jesus, please be his stay
Thank You that You will.

As times get tough and dark
And his petals fold in
The prayer from our hearts is
Let Your sunshine flood his soul
Make Neil well and whole
As You do this
Sap will flow through and fill his stem
He shall bloom for You again!

And as time passes by
His petals will fade and fall
His plant shrivelled, becoming a lifeless seed
For time in eternity
He shall then fall into the ground
His lifeless seed.

But Lord, a seed has to die to live
Our prayer then for Neil is
As his roots thrust down into the soil
A sturdy tree will grow, tall and strong
Reaching out and up to You.

In fullness his branches will extend
Bearing blooms and fruit for God and friend
A shade and comfort be
To all scorched from heat
Animals will rest in his roots
Birds shall nest on his branches' ends
A comfort he will be, for all his friends.

Lord, as we look at our son
Your lovely young bud
Show him what he will be
A strong and sturdy tree in eternity
Where time never parts or ends.

Thank You, Father, for Neil
Our precious son!

IS IT ENOUGH?

It is enough to be weak
It is enough to be beautiful
It is enough to love
It is enough to reach for the stars.

For God
Is my portion and my strength
He is my morning star
God is beautiful and He is love.

And to live is to have my being in God
And that is enough!

GOD IS SEEN

God, the blue sky
God of the green earth
Thank You for breathing life into me.

God of the red flower
God of the lashing seas
God of the moving tide
Thank You for breathing life into me.

God of the mountains
In purple splendour hue
God of the majestic trees
I love You.

God of the bumblebee
God of the tiniest ant
God of all creeping creatures
God of the smallest and living plant
Bless You for breathing life into me.

God of the universe
You spoke the works and creation took place
Bless You, for Your hand fashioned me.

Holy Spirit and Eternal
God, my Father
May my life
Breath of Your life
Magnify Your Name.

A PLACE FOR YOU

I've a special place for you, my friend
Whose friendship is loyal and true
Can I say what you mean to me?
Can I say how dear you've become to me?
You've grown and entwined
Deep in my heart
I'm glad our friendship
Was right from the start.

My special friend, as I look to you
I would like to say
Thanks for your prayers every day
Thanks for protecting me in every way
Thanks for putting me first in our friendship.

Deep and tender is the love that I express
Deep and tender is the love that I have
Deep and tender it continues to grow.

So, my wonderful friend
Take my love and take my prayers
Take my thoughts
All from one who deeply cares
Draw them with the bond of my love
Depend on me, my loyalty is yours
A sure guarantee!

For I shall never desert
I shall never cause hurt or pain
To the one who is so special to me
I shall encourage and I shall care for you
I shall build a fortress of love around you
I shall protect and I shall defend
I shall be faithful to life's end
My friend, take all that I offer you.

My friend, I ask only one thing from you
My friend, never ever change
I love you, just the way you are.

ALL I ASK, DEAR LORD

All I ask, dear Lord
Is to hear Your voice to me
An individual in Galilee
My faith has made me well.

Now I can go in peace
For, dear Lord, You spoke the words
That healed me
Praise God, as I at Your feet fall
My praise I bring as I give to You my all.

LIVE FOR JESUS

Live for Jesus, each fresh new day
Let Him hold over your being, absolute sway
Let Him fill, glorify and use all that you do
Keeping your eyes fixed on our heavenly home.

Live for Jesus, each fresh new day
Desiring to care for all His creation
Given to your hand
Be still in your soul, dying to the temporal
Live for the eternal, bringing pleasure to our God.

Yes, let pleasure indeed
Fill our Father's heart as He sees you
Set yourself apart
For use as His instrument.

Live for Jesus, each fresh new day
Let Him hold over your being, absolute sway.

THOUGHTS ABOUT YOU

I was thinking about you
My friend, faithful and true
Well, almost - no one is perfect, hey!
But still you were there, when I needed care.

Time passes, life goes on
Relationships change
Maturing or disappearing
Ours disappeared and matured
And was caught up in swells of life and of living
But the cord is still strong, threefold strong
Secure against the storms of time.

Storms, earthquakes and seasons
All mine and all yours
Yet we still belong to the cord of love
Ever living and ever strong.

Do we really understand, I wonder?
Do you understand?
The things that cannot be said
They would need to be undone
Bringing a loosening
Of our ties.

I do not want you to say anything
For dreams will be scattered
And a fragment of time, precious to me
Will fray, leaving jagged edges
That will not smooth away.

Yet in the same way, talk
Reach out with hands and eyes
Touch and see all that there is left unsaid.

I get scared, you know - do you?
I wonder at the wonder of it all
It is beautiful and deep like a melody
It has no sides, no depth and no end, I pray.

I hope in you, for you are strong to hold me
And I need you just as you are
Part of me and part of you, blended into one
Yet unknowing what we know
And not knowing the unknown.

My friend, be there for in the depths, there is love
Blossoming and unfailing 'til the end of time
Fragile and tender in shortness of life.

Breath, grant that I may breathe
A gentle rhythm as onward I go
In light, love and contentment
Lead us on, separate yet together
Until our breath becomes one
Like the wind, forever free.

SHADOWS

Standing in the shadows
God is there with me
Standing in the shadows
God's will is there for me.

He will uphold and keep
He will press me to His bosom
Standing in the shadows, I fear nothing there
For God, my Father, in tender mercy and grace
Is also standing there.

Standing in the shadows
I worship my Father above
Standing in the shadows
I am kept by His love
And in His perfect timing
And in His perfect grace
The shadows move ten steps away from me.

Until then, I may weep bitterly
And cry out to my God
He hears and sees my tears
And I know, though the shadows still remain
My Father's love is still the same.

Now the shadows no longer scare
For in the shadows
I am resting, resting in His care.

THE WINTER TREE

The bare tree said to nature, "Why do you not adorn me?
Why am I naked for all to see - have you no clothes to
cover my shame?
Where is my fruit and why no fragrant bower?
Why do you treat me this way, revealing my dry frame?

"My shame is enough for me
And I am placed alongside healthy trees
That blossom and bear fruit on every branch
And are weighed down with their usefulness.

"I am in the midst of this greenery
I shudder at the thought that there is no use for me
Dry and brittle
Look at me, nature's shame."

Nature replied, "Why do you question
A natural season for a healthy tree?
Why do you compare yourself in a winter season
Against others in a summer season?
Can you not look to my blue sky
And clouds of endless and perfect days?

"You are part of this, a place prepared for you
Will you listen to the music that nature makes in
completion And take your place in this symphony of
glory?
Look not to yourself, for is not the sap of life within?

"At the right time this sap will arise and flood your being
And all the dry wood and dead leaves will fall away
In their place, growth

And green, fresh new buds will break forth.
They will compliment you with fragrant flowers
In time these will change to fruit for all to see.

"This life is there and will surely rise within you
Being under control of my hand
Shall not your fruitfulness be all the more beautiful
Due to the contrast against the starkness of your winter
season?
You are useful to me and we are part of each other
This life may be dormant but it is there, awaiting the
season.

"One thing I ask of you, winter tree
When the sap rises, will you resist or yield to this growth
And give your all to its purpose?
A tree that resists has stunted growth
But a tree that yields bears fruit one hundredfold.

"Look again and you shall see that I have my purpose and
plan
A tree cannot always understand
So question not, but remain part of me
And I, nature, will make you into an everlasting tree
Of beauty beyond compare
A tree that will be remembered forever.

"In your youth, you shall be cut down
To bear Him with thorns for a crown
You will be the tree that carries and supports life Himself
This is my purpose for you, a tree weighed down in
winter time To be the tree of perfect time
Remembered in your beauty, ages past to ages come."

Tree of Calvary, take your place
To bear your Saviour's weight
Oh! Season of Pain
You are not a dead tree
For the Saviour touches you
Resurrection life flows
You are perfect, part of Him
Glorified for eternity.

DEGRADATION

In the depth of degradation
God's love is for me
In the depth of vengeance
God's love is for me
In the depth of desire
God's love is for me
In the depth of rebellion
God's love is for me
In the depth of despair
God's love is for me
In the depth of disobedience
God's love is for me
In the depth of all hurt and sin
God's love is for me
In the depth of love and sacrifice
God's love is for me.

God, my Father, what amazing love
I thank and I praise You
That I cannot shake off Your devotion for me.

ARTIFICIAL LIMB

I do not want to be
An artificial limb for Thee
Yet to be whole, complete and still
Doing Your work with love and skill
Winning souls for You
Feeding Your lambs, too
Abiding and bearing fruit for You
For this I need
Fullness, availability and stability
A life committed completely.

Is this me, a live and living part of the body?
Moving in rhythm with the other parts?
Joined in the Head, functioning as a whole?

Who is our Head? His Name is Jesus!
So I turn to You, and Father, I ask You
For tender grace as I pilgrim on with Your son
To that place called home
By Your grace, let me be
Total and committed, a working, living limb in Thee.

OUR MUM!

I've never written a poem for you, Mum
I've never got around to getting things done
God's given me a wonderful gift
Expressing in writing how I feel and live
God, my Father, also gave me a wonderful Mum
Strong, able and lots of fun.

Consistent and lovingly strict, too
Understandable, looking at your children too!
We must have given you a hard time
Many times, stepping out of line
I know, and Mum, forgive us!
But this poem is not to look at me
It's for my Mum, who God gave to me!

Who else would have persevered so
With her heavy burden and load?
You worked hard every day
So that we could grow up in every way
Many times, you must have wanted to scream and shout
Then pull your hair out!
But Mum, you stuck to your guns when the pressure was
on
God gave us a fantastic Mum!

You worked hard and yet had time to play
Mum, do you remember the times we were gay
Skipping, running and jumping too
Mum, we learned a lot from you!

We learned to have fun through it all
Because you taught us this, we now have a ball!
How to be consistent through all
Through thick and thin, never giving in at all.

Your strength of character is for us
An example to follow through eternity
I thank God for that wonderful day
He knew which Mum to put our way
Things were never perfect all the time
But Mum, you did have hard times.

One thing, Mum, I remember about you
Is how you loved your children
Through all those tender and hard years
Another thing I remember about you
You loved to suck your little finger, too
Mum, where did you get that habit from?
Mum, it would have been wiser to suck your thumb!

Well, my poem nears its end
But not my love for our Mum and our friend!
God bless and keep you, and though we're far apart
Never forget, Mum, you have that place in our heart
A place so special and tender is there
For our Mum who's always cared with a tear!
Your treasure is us, your children
Our treasure is you!
Mum, today God shall bless our treasure, YOU!

A STORM

I'm in the middle of the storm, Lord
I feel safe and calm
I'm in Your everlasting arms
I'm secure and I'm quiet
The storm rages but cannot hurt
This tiny creation is trusting in You.

I will come through the raging fury
Lord, I want to bring You glory
Your desire for me is that I look to You
Perfect rest and perfect love
Is sent from heaven above
I'm casting all care onto You
Safely in the storm and I'm coming through.

FEARFUL

When the world falls around you
And fears and doubts surround you
When you are fearful
And storm clouds gather, ready to burst
Remember that God cares.

He will never leave you
His love will enfold you
So rest in His tender care
For He is watching from above.

Come, my child, rest in my love
I will hold you and tenderly enfold you
Taking you through the storm
Lean on my everlasting arms.

My child, you have been spiritually born
Placed in my family
Never doubt, never fear
I Am is always near
Trust and be still living in Me
And I, your Father
Will see you through.

DESIRE FOR GOD

Lord, make me a living Flame
Drawing Sinners to Your Name
The joy of an abundant Life
Can be theirs, through strife.

As they walk with God's Son
Along life's road
Onward bound they shall be
To the Father in Eternity.

How joyful and peaceful
In the midst of the storm
And we shall come Home
To our Father's Arms.

Welcome and clean we shall ever be
Wrapped in God's arms for Eternity.

BREAKDOWN

Alone and in despair
Fear and anxiety, no one cares
My mind is warped
With uncontrollable thoughts
That cause me to live within myself.

Scars mark my thoughts and emotions
I despair that I will never get over them
So I hide within myself
I lose contact with reality
My mind starts to break down
I try to keep calm
I cannot explain, I cannot talk
And prefer people to stay away from me
For I am frightened they will see
The darker side of me
This will frighten them
For they cannot understand.

But there is one who can
His name, the Lord Jesus Christ
He has been there before
Feeling agony and despairingly forlorn.

His mind was also torn in two
He had to choose Himself on the tree
To die for you and me
Angels could have set Him free
In the middle of His agony
He chose to stay in perfect obedience
To the Father's will
Knowing He would bear on the cross
Our deepest despairs and utter loss.

He suffered in the garden
How deeply, we will never know
All the forces of evil were there
Oppressing Him to total despair
His sweat was like drops of blood
The love He had for us would
Win over the fear
Of separation from His Father.

He won the battle that day
And now He lives to pray each day
At the Father's right hand
Pleading for us that we will also stand
Those evil satanic onslaughts
Against our minds and bodies.

We will stand
Because we are blood bought
Jesus will never let us go
No matter what our problems are
Jesus is with us, so we need not despair.

He can heal mind and body
According to His will as we are still
We must listen to Him each day
Letting the Spirit have His way
Giving Him complete control.

Then minds and emotions shall rest in Him
Preparing us for the fight again
He knows every step of the way
He has trod there before
He will help us onward bound
He will always be around
Need we fear? Sometimes we do
But these are the times
That God's Promises claimed come true.

My Father, You are my most precious possession
I long to be complete with You in heaven
Until that day, keep my mind on You
Showing me the work that I must do.

Thank You that I have in You
A strength and shield for the battle ahead
Refresh my mind with thoughts of You.

Praise You, Jesus, that You do understand
And will hold me forever in Your Hands
Never let me fade or fall
For I have given to You my all.

TEACH ME, JESUS

Teach me, Jesus, the old way
Like a spring within, in a newer way
Teach me, Jesus, the old way
Through the pain and tears again.

Teach me, Jesus, in a new way
And as eternal springs rise within
Each fresh new day
Let Your Spirit within me glow
Reaping harvest fields for You alone
Use all that comes my way
As I hide in You, praying Father to You
Abiding and resting in You, ever new.

Teach me, Father, the old way
As I'm cleansed in Your holy tide
As I rest in Your Holy place
As I pray and think things through
Jesus, help me hide in You
Hold my anchor fast in the Rock of Calvary.

Teach me, Father, the old way
Resting in Your holy temple
In Calvary's Christ, Your precious side
Wounded for me.

THE FUTURE FOR ME

The future for me is dark and bleak
I only know that you, Lord are there
That is my guarantee.

No matter what happens in this life
I shall trust You all the way
Knowing I haven't got a great faith
But one thing I do know
Is that You love me so
And all You expect of me
Is faith, the size of a mustard seed.

My small faith trusts in my great God
Who once trod this earth
Walking, talking, and sleeping on the sod.

I know with certainty that You will bring me through
Because of Your love and my trust in You
You are utterly dependable and trustworthy
So I give You praise and glory.

I fear and doubt but I will not give in
For Your eternal arms are around me again, Amen
No matter how dark or bleak the path ahead
I will never let You go, for Jesus, I love You so!

VALENTINE

I want you for my Valentine
Because in my heart you shine
This is a very special day
When I am allowed to say
You are the most wonderful guy.

Deep within me I sigh, *Why?*
You switch me completely on
I adore being with you, having fun
In all the experiences of life
Loving and talking, sharing and walking
I love you in the silence, too
What more can I say, Valentine?

One day, say you will be mine
Yes or no, tell me so
If yes, then my heart shall soar like a dove
And I can rest completely in your love
Valentine, please be mine
From - guess who?
The one who really loves you!

A PRAYER

Help me believe, You can restore and heal
As I rest in You completely
No matter how long it takes
Instantaneously, or gradually
I accept Your will for my life
Gladly knowing that You are the one
Who laid down His life for me.

I do trust in Your eternal love
Because the bible tells me so
That You, my Lord, will never let me go
Let me live my life in You
Knowing You are taking me through
To the mansions in heaven above
Where I shall rest, eternally in Your love.

MY FEELINGS

How do I feel today
After this pressure?
My Lord went through this
Only far worse for Him.

The cost was His life on the Tree
His friendship with His disciples
Could never be the same again
After He had risen
He had to leave them
Parted in the body, from those He loved
Taken back to God's loving and welcome arms.

God then sent forth the Holy Spirit
He came to teach and restrain, help and comfort
All those who loved Jesus.

That's what happened in my life
The Holy Spirit came
Through the dark and doubting fears
Bringing comfort and calm
As He wrapped me in His arms.

Now I'm assured of my place above
Because of my Father's wonderful love
Holy Spirit, magnify the name of Jesus
Hallelujah to the King of Glory!

I'M FREE

I shall listen and I shall believe
I shall act, for I am free
Free in Christ, yet chained in love
To be merciful and not to judge.

With the Spirit's power
Lord, in my freedom, help me
To be committed to Your cause eternally
You have shown me mercy
So help me by Your wonderful grace
To act and live for You
Giving glory to our Father above.

CHANGES

The caterpillar went for a walk
And saw his fellow man
He went beneath bushes and roots
And never to the sky
Did his eye scan.

Somewhere a prayer was made
And along came the chrysalis stage
Emerging with steady breathing
A little effort on his part
A stretching of his wing span
A rise and a jump, then off he goes
He's a butterfly, you know!

He wings his way high above the earth
Seeing trees and flowers below
The mountains he scans, and rivers too
What delights await you!

Colour and cloud with endless day
Sun and pleasure each day with play
Zipping and diving in the air
Winging on the breadth of a prayer
Oh! Yes, a butterfly I be
For Jesus came to set me free to fly!

HIS NAME!

I dare not mention
His Name!
There is so much Authority in
His Name!
Glory and Power belong to
His Name!
The devil flees in
His Name!
We are partakers of Divinity, thanks to
His Name!
All that thrills my soul is
His Name!
Higher, greater than any other
His Name!
Oh, Blessed Name upon my lips
His Name!
Hallelujah, Praise and Glory to
His Name!
What a privilege is mine, thanks to
His Name!
In confidence I can whisper
His Name!
A name so divine
I worship and I praise, Jesus!

REBELLION

Why do I rebel against You, Lord
When things go wrong?
My desire for prayer, it disappears
I have no listening ears
My desire for Your Word dwindles
The spark of fire no longer kindles in my heart.

I feel hurt and despondent
Removed from Grace
And yet I know that this is not the case
You are faithful and I am faithless.

You are unchanging and I am changing
You will not let me go
No matter what pace or place I go.

Hold me tight, Lord
Forgive my selfish plea
Lord, I'm always asking things for Me
Help me desire to know Your Will
Giving You Praise and keeping myself still
Knowing You do understand
The fight going on inside of me.

You will never leave me
I must fellowship with You again
For deep within
The Spirit calls me back again
Praise You, Jesus, and Amen.

DAVE AND JAYNE

I have two precious friends, dear Lord
And in their hearts You are adored
You have led them all the way
And I thank You for that day
When their path with mine was entwined.

Their love and help in my time of need
Has in my life planted a seed of love
Which for them shall always grow, expanding
Until fulfilled when we abide in Thee.

Right now, they need You, Lord
Your path has become a maze
Perhaps they feel trapped in a cage
I pray You will set their spirits free
So that they can worship Thee.

Help them to love, adore and trust
And know Your plan and way
Will be made plain one day
As they continue and abide in You.

Dave and Jayne, in the Lord
I love you!

HOSPITAL STAY

We are patients in the hospital
Our sport here, we climb the wall
Our doctors drive us berserk
Upon examination
They cause us pain and hurt.

Pills, pills and medicine galore
But the injections hurt far more
The doctors rub their hands in glee
As we suffer here patiently
They see the pain on our faces
And think we're mental cases
If the truth were only known
They would leave us all alone.

In the morning the doctors come
To prod and poke, having their fun
They then leave us for the rest of the day
Having had plenty to say
We're left in the very capable hands
Of the Sisters and nurses here
That cause us tremendous fear.

We know what happens when our doctor's gone
We laugh and giggle and have our fun
The nurses would like us to be still
Because of their patients, they've had their fill!

Actually, we patients care a lot for you
Doctors, Sisters and nurses too
Keep on doing your good work
And we will see you again one day
Until then, we hope you get a rise in pay!

WALKING AHEAD, NOT IN FANTASY

Walking ahead, not in fantasy
But in the reality of life
With its pain and strife
Joy and sweetness, too.

Jesus, I love You so much
For Your great faithful willingness
To obtain my salvation, full and free.

My Father, as I walk along
May my life reflect the song
Of that salvation, full and free
Praise You that I belong to Your Son.

QUESTIONING

Lord, there is so much that I don't understand
And yet I know You're still holding my hand
I feel heaven's door is closed in my face
Yet You have promised
I am one of Your chosen race.

Oh! To give my life fully to You
It sounds such an easy thing to do
Yet, there is the flesh fighting on
Being helped by Satan and his throng.

You have promised me victory, Lord
From self and sin, set me free
For there is work to be done
Saving souls for Your Son.

People need You, I feel that I'm wasting time
Forgive me, cleanse me
Fill me and use me
For the glory of Your Son
Then use my time for Thee
Winning souls who will be with You in eternity.

YOUR WORK AND MY PAIN

Jesus, there is so much hurt within my soul
Yet You died to make me whole
You rose again in victory
To take away my misery
My actions were full of folly
I see that I did not trust You fully
I seem to be losing ground
Even though You are around.

But I know through these experiences
You will bring me through
My small faith clings to You
I remember that You have promised me
You are with me now and through eternity.

So taking a firm stand
Refusing my feelings, the better hand
Onward bound I shall walk and talk with You
For Lord, I do love and need You.

Thank You that You're by my side
Against the lashing waves and moving tide
Of emotions that will not be still
Until You, Lord, reign on the throne of my life.

Take my pain and strife
Then full of peace I shall be
As I look into Your gracious face
Cleansed and calm I shall be.

Perfect peace, God is good
Together the storm we stood
And now I am resting in Your love.

THANK YOU FOR THE GOOD TIMES

Thank You for the good times in my life, Lord
Enjoying my life, given from Your Hand
So that I can learn from these experiences
How great and wonderful You are
Making precious moments
To store tight in my memories.

In the same breath
Thank You for the bad times in my life, Lord
Those times of hurt and pain
That bring sadness to my memories
Finding comfort with You.

As Your love to me drew a response which I can say
I'm learning to live on life's way
Through it You do understand
And lead me on to the promised land
Thank You for comfort and, God, for being You.

SADNESS AND JOY

Looking past the sadness and the joy
My spiritual eyes see
Jesus Christ glorified, living in You
Walk with me, our eyes lifted up
There are no limits to our spiritual walk
We want to tread that path and see our Lord.

Our eyes searching ever
To see His wondrous face
And when we fix our eyes upon Him
By His power and grace
With thanksgiving in our hearts and full of praise
Wonder and love, we shall be praising Jesus
Who has lifted you and me!

So come walk with me to deeper living realms
Where Jesus controls the helm!
Thank You, Jesus, that You are alive
And allow us by faith
To see You with our eyes!

YOUTH

Young healthy bodies
Young healthy minds
Furthering the cause of Christ
For mankind
May our children be cleansed
And in fellowship with You
Furthering the Father's cause
Drawing sinners to Your Son.

By Your power and by Your Grace
Give them strength to win the race
Where they will at life's end
Look into the Father's face
Radiant and without spot
Perfectly cleansed, not a single blot.

Ever grateful they shall be
To Jesus for His faithful ministry
He is praying at God's right Hand
That their faith shall not fall, but stand
They will stand because Jesus prays for them
Thank You, Lord Jesus, our life's end.

MY DAD

If I kiss you, my Dad, lips to lips
A fine parting it would be
But if I kiss you from my heart
This proves we're never apart
For where God is, there is you
For where God is, there is me.

He with us
And us with Him
Never a parting to be
And so, I kiss you from my heart
Can you tell this kiss apart?
It is a kiss in Him
Whose love knows no end
And in Him
We will never part.

He has made a place for us
Perfect and together in His heart!
So take this kiss from *my* heart
It is for you, my Dad!

GROW

The work of Your Hand is me
A sapling, longing to be a tree
For You.
Nourish my soul
That I may grow
Tend the work of Your Hand
Bringing fruit from this precious plant
And as the fruit matures
Falling ripe to the ground
Let others taste the flesh
And in You be blessed.

Let the seeds go forth, multiplying
One hundredfold for You
May other saplings grow
At the side of this healthy tree.
My child,
You shall grow and mature
Bearing fruit one hundredfold
Multiplying at My source
Blessings then shall go forth
Glory shall be brought to My Name
I shall tend the work of My Hands.

Continue growing in this earth
No longer barren
Earth that is no longer cursed
But blessed in righteousness
Due to My Son's willingness
To die on a tree
Bringing forth eternal fruit
Due to His obedience.

He also bore fruit one hundredfold
For the work of My Hands
Touched that lifeless tree
And became the earth's blessing for eternity.

My child, obedience is the key
To being a healthy, fruitful tree.

MY WORRY

I've just had some bad news, Lord
And it boils down to: Will You take care of me
forevermore?
Will You provide for all my needs?
I'm fearful to tread the path of faith
Can I fully trust the keeper of the gate?

My faith flounders
As I look at the waves and storms of life ahead of me
Shall I be able to keep still, trusting You finally
Until I see You face to face?

Dearest child, I died for your fear and strife
I came and identified with you
Living, I also went through pain
I was a carpenter, until I was thirty
And for three years until my death
I totally relied on my Father
He took care of me, never letting me down
He was always around, providing for my needs.

We shall also take care of you
Because we love and adore you
We've made a way for you to completely trust and be still
Unquenchable is the source, so trust to us your cause
We shall take care of you forevermore!

FILL ME WITH YOUR SPIRIT, LORD

Fill me with Your Spirit, Lord
So that in my life, You are adored
Help me fight evil with Your Word
Hold me close with love's strong cord.

Let the world's loss be Your gain
And then with the angels my voice will sing
Forever, Jesus is Lord and King!

TRUST

Your trust in me, Father, is unbelievable
How shall I respond?
I must give You my free will daily
As I seek Your face
Give me the supporting grace
To pray not my will, but Thine be done.

Break me and mould me then fill me
Use me as Your instrument
To guide and love people as You did
Bringing them comfort from Your word
Assuring them that Your work finished on the cross.

Will You do this and use a sinner like me?
Because of Jesus
Yes, You will as daily I seek
To give You my free will
By Your supporting grace.

REMEMBER ME

All I ask of you is to remember me loving you
Forget the pain and wrong attitudes
Remember me loving you
Forget what I've said that's caused tremendous hurt
Remember me encouraging you
Forget the times I've strayed from our friendship's way
Instead, hold me close in the bond of memories
Loving you.

Smile once in a while as you think of my actions
Loving you
Forget my wrong reactions, so very strong
Just remember me loving you
And once in a while, as time goes by
Remember me hurting for you
Because I love you.

WHY

Dear loving and compassionate Lord Jesus
Will You tell me why?

Remain not silent as the tears flow by
Still I suffer, and in Your tender care
I know that if I come
I will find a solace in prayer.

My rebel heart plans a way
Like a foolish and stupid sheep, I go astray
Yet Your loving hand is there to guide me
Holding, loving and comforting me
At times of these blessings, I am unaware
Because the pressure is so hard to bear.

Dear loving, compassionate Lord Jesus
Will You tell me why?

My prayers seem to go unheard
And yet I know that You have heard
All I pray, feel and think, all bring me to the brink
Of losing hold of my Saviour's hand
I feel that my life is built on sand
Help me to hide in Your precious, bleeding side
And one day I will know the reason why.

MAKE TIME FOR GOD'S KINGDOM

Make time for God's Kingdom
Make time for God and His word
Fight evil and sin continually
With His powerful word.

Make time for yourself
To be what He wants you to be
Make time for God's children
Meeting their spiritual need
Stepping out in the watchful care
Of His Holy Spirit
Witness, breathe and live Jesus
Telling all you know
About your wonderful friend.

Make time for glory and honour
Make time for His Kingdom
Make time for Jesus
King for eternity
Make time and spend time with Jesus
Life's best friend.

A BATTLE

There's a great battle
Going on in my soul
I want You, Lord
Yet at the same time
What do I want? I don't know.

Yet the struggle goes on
I feel torn between myself and Your Son
What shall I do?
I know I love You
Yet there is a part of me that will not give in.

I pray, fight for me, Lord
Help me to turn to Your Word
Give me the desire to seek deep, hidden truths
Finding out more about You
And as I do this, help me to lose
The grasping hand of self.

I will give You praise and glory
As You take complete control
Then and only then will the struggle cease
And in my soul, I will receive peace.

SEASONS

When spring comes down this way
Bringing flowers oh so gay
With their sweet and gentle smell
Bringing beauty to every dell.

Summer comes with skies so blue
And birds that like to bill and coo
The clouds are fluffy and shining white
With days that stretch into the night.

Autumn with colours brown and gold
Has a story to be told
The leaves begin to fall
And winter now starts to call.

The thrill of the very first sight
Of the clean snow so white
Winter now so long is here
But spring around the corner is near.

AFTER GETHSEMANE

After Gethsemane
The cost for Jesus
His life on the Tree
His friendship with the disciples
Could never be the same again
After He had risen, He had to leave them
Parted in the body from those He loved
Yet still caring for them.

Taken back to God's loving Arms
Then God sent forth the Holy Spirit
He came to teach and restrain
Help and comfort again
All those who love Jesus.

That's what happened in my dark day
The Holy Spirit came
Through the dark and doubting fears
Bringing comfort and calm
As He wrapped me in my Father's arms.

Now I'm assured of my place above
Because of my Father's wonderful love
Holy Spirit, magnify Jesus' Name
Truly wonderful is my story
Hallelujah to the King of Glory.

FOR PENNY AND BARBARA

Lord, strengthen my heart
Now the pain begins to start
Lord, forgive me for being myself
Hurting when it comes to parting.

I blame You, Lord, for my pain
I cry, Oh Lord, I need You
The pressure is hard to bear
Because of the friendship we share.

Help me, Lord, to say goodbye
Remembering it's only for a little while
We will all meet again on this earth
And then finally, in Your Arms
There will be no more pain
We shall all be together again
The body, as One in you
Our Living Head.

STAY BY ME

Don't go away, please stay - why?
Because
You're my ice cream on a hot summer's day
You're my fire on a cold winter's night
You're my apple when I tick
You're my doctor when I'm sick
You're my water when I'm thirsty
You're my tear when I cry
When I feel better, you're my sigh.

You're my rainbow in the rain
Without you, life will never be the same
You're my sunshine in the clouds
Break through and shine right now
You're the child within my soul
With you I feel complete and whole
When I'm down you raise me up.

Without you, what will I do?
For darling, I need you!

ENDURING

Endure the faith and run the race
To the finishing line
Into eternity's time
You have for me
The prize of victory.

I will then see Your graceful face
As I complete the race
Righteousness is mine
Thanks to Jesus the Divine
Oh! What joy is in store
With Our Father forevermore.

ANGER

Anger, springing up from hurt and frustration
It would be easy to lose control
And give in to fear, hurt and sin
My emotions swell like a tide
I try to control them
If not, I hide them.

Deep within myself
I fear I will give in
To the pain and consequence of my sin
I need You, Lord Jesus Christ
Help me give to You
All the hurt, frustration and pain
Help me in my heart
To release Your Spirit, Lord
To cleanse and fill the empty void.

And in faith I will give You Praise
For what You are going to do
Lord Jesus Christ, I'm trusting You.

MY TEMPLE MUST NOT BE

My Temple must not be
A den of iniquity
Before I, the Son
Can make you shine
You must be willing to forsake sin
Then being illumined and cleansed
I shall shine forth from thee.

Then my witness you shall be
Spiritually alive
The glow reflecting in your eyes
You will not see this, my child
Because then my glory will be quenched
As you become full of self.

But others will see Jesus living in thee
Bringing praise to my name
Because self you overcame
By the Holy Spirit working in you
The life of Jesus shall be seen in you.

LIFE WITH GOD SHALL BE

Life with God shall be
In God's dwelling place, eternally
Old things have passed away
God is our light, night and day.

So I set my face towards the Son
Lord, lead me on to the promised land
Where God is, there shall I be.

LESSONS

I want to learn through my suffering, Lord
I want glory brought to Your name
Teach me the value of pain
For You went through the same.

In the darkness, Your light shines
Bringing Your comfort felt so dear
For You, Lord, are very near.

Boldly I shall stand at the gate
Knowing You are there
My certainty of my place in heaven is Jesus.

Father, You are so wonderful
I am so small
Help me to love You, and give You my all.

My praise, my love and my life
I shall give to Jesus
Who has set me free to live and love.

AM I A FOOL?

Sometimes I think I am a fool
Dare I say it, for worshipping You
Because You are like no other God
You hold me with love's strong chain
Drawing me to Your side again
And from that love, I cannot turn away
I resist and I fight, but there is no other way
I keep on turning towards Your Son.

Your love for me has a magnetic hold
Your love for me never grows cold
How can I fight You, Lord?
Turning my back on such a precious truth
That Your love will never fade away
Your love keeps me, day by day.

Though at times I do fight and resist
I have to turn around
For in love's strong chain I am bound
A prisoner for life in You
No longer a fool, for You love me as no other can
Father and Holy Spirit, thank You for Your Son.

MAY THE LORD BLESS YOU

May the Lord bless you
And the showers of His love refresh you
Cascading down from above
Sent by the Father in His love.

Sprinkled by Him, unseen
Washing and keeping us clean
By the Holy Spirit's power
Let the showers fall this hour.

In return we shall give praise and glory
Through Jesus, the son
To Our Father who has made us one!

EMOTIONAL TURMOIL

Shock leads to rejection
Then comes the loss of affection
Leading to depression
Continuing on to isolation in one's self
Next is guilt, brought on by frustration
Bound in hurt
Through situations beyond one's control.

Self-acceptance is next to go
Fear walks in the open door
Panic, too, comes this way
Existing to live becomes the way
Frozen feelings keep the pain away
One is unstable in every way
Communication has now gone
The road in emotional turmoil seems very long.

But help can come from a source
And barriers start to break down
As someone shows they care
Anger then comes and takes control
Fierce determination now rises in the soul
New feelings now take control
Panic and fear are thrown out of the door
Frozen tears start springing to the fore
Self-acceptance then starts to grow
Barriers break down fast
Guilt is now here, near the last.

But in searching for a friend who cares
This is the next step to healing tears
Sharing every step of the way
Isolation now goes away
Depression, then, is the next
For this takes time and many tears
A battle fought with many fears.

Then that friend's affection shared
Sorts out rejection, one's no longer as scared
At last, facing the shock and the emotional block
The barriers are completely down
Healing tears continue to spring forth
For comfort found with that friend
Starts the road to recovery again.

Life new begins
The pain and hurt becoming part of you
Fresh strength with communication
Stemming from that vital love
One learns to love and to give again
Through hurt and pain
We are beginning to live again.

LIVING FOR GOD

Living for Jesus, day by day
In His presence I must lay
Accepting the fullness that He brings
So my heart for Him shall sing.

Oh! Love shed abroad in my Heart
Help me to tell others the simple plan
That You set forth, through the Son of Man
All may come to Him and belong
On repentance to Him, the Son of God
Receive and believe and we are set free
From sin holding us captive.

Then, in joy so full
That words cannot express
Father, thank You and praise You
For the plan You've made
So that I could return to You
Abide, rest and adore You
Oh! The fullness from above
As I believe in Your love.

Accepted and free, we shall ever be
Praising our Father, through Eternity
Eternity is now this gracious hour
Thank You, Holy Spirit, for Your power
To praise Father, through Jesus the Son.

In confidence we can say
We trust You more each day
And look forward to that day
When at last, face to face
We shall see You by Your Grace.

Help us run the race
Looking to our Father
Setting our sights on Heaven above
Where we shall rest
Eternally in Your love.

POEM OF GOD

I am the Poem of God
As He in Christ created me
The fullness of His word
Assures this fact to me
We, the poem of God... little 'ole me?

He loves to take 'nothing'
So His beauty may be seen
He expressed Himself willingly
A beauteous thing beyond compare
And out of His bounteous Grace
A poem I became!

Oh! Let your love through me flow
That it might be seen
If God can make a poem of me
He can do it for you, too
Have you met this Grace
Told in Christ?

CROWN HIM AND HAIL HIM

Crown Him and Hail Him, King Jesus
Serve, follow and suffer
For Jesus, your Lord and King.

Crown Him King
Hail Him innocent Lamb of God
Prepared to die for you to Crown Him.

Crown Him with Joy
Anoint His Head
Once crowned with thorns for you.

Crown Him with service
As He served you
Crown Him with your life
As He once gave His life
For you.

Crown Him with obedience
Crown Him with love
The King of love, who died loving you.

Crown Him Master and God
Hail Him and praise Him
King Jesus, Lord of all life
Creator of all being
We crown and worship You.

WORSHIP

All the world will proclaim
The beauty of Your name
All the world will confess
Jesus is the Son of Righteousness.

I am to bow before You
I will share in Your glory too
Seated with You
In heavenly places.

As I walk this path below
Let the beauty of Jesus flow
With power and strength to help
And grace to quench myself.

To share Your Glory
I must become like You
Giving of my free will
Taking on the nature of a servant
Being humble and walking in obedience to the cross
Bringing death to my nature.

This done, I'm raised by Your Son
To my place above
Thank You, Father
Precious Son
Through Your Spirit
For Your love.

THE SHADOW OF HIS WINGS

Living under the shadow of His Wings
Giving praise and glory to my King
Resting in His holy place
Restored by His Bountiful Grace.

Living under the shadow of His Wings
Complete, filled and whole I become
Receiving joy from the Son
Lifting the name of Jesus higher
Under the shadow of His Wings.

Most Holy blessed Place
Gazing into Jesus' face
Under the shadow of the Everlasting Wings
I worship You, my God and King.

PRAISE FOR THE KING

Hosannah to the King
In prison, my prison?
Maybe in your prison but not mine.

Hosannah to the King
Lifting voice in praise
Acknowledging His grace
In prison?
Heartaches, sorrow, tears and fears
Imprisoned?
Freedom, I cry
Then I will praise
But not with lock on prison gate.

Hosannah to the King
Who has the key
To set me free
Yet allows the chains to remain.

Hosannah to the King
Lifting up my head
Joy and delight filling my soul
In darkness, locked in jail?

Hosannah to the King
I am known in Christ
Renewing faith and hope
To those outside
Can this be
Service in prison for Thee?

Hosannah to the King
I will praise and serve Him
My King
In prison
Until He sets me free
Eternally.

Hosannah to my King
Praise him!

PRAISE

At work and at play I want to say
Praise Jesus!
As I dust, wash and clean
Through my spiritual eyes
Let Jesus be seen.

In health and joy, love and peace
Let my praise never cease
In sadness and sickness and in pain
Let my hope in You not be in vain
Praise Jesus!

MR BENJAMIN

To Mr. Benjamin
I've never met you
I only know that you're a Jew
That is enough for me to say
In Jesus, I love you!

You know, you are very precious in His sight
By His blood you've been set right
With God, who has chosen your race
To take care of His Holy Book.

Please, Mr. Benjamin
Won't you take a good look in that wonderful book?
You will see that Jesus, the Messiah
Died for you as well as me.

I pray by His Grace, you will come to Him
For the Lion of Judah is gently calling you in
He desires that you become a completed Jew in Him
Oh! Mr Benjamin, because of Yeshua, I love you!

DEAR SISTER

Strive not, my dear sister, strive not
Enter into rest and strive not
He will keep and never fail
He will hold through sunshine and hail.

Strive not, my dear sister, strive not
Jesus paid the full price, so strive not
He initiated your salvation
He shall complete the same
His promises are true.

Strive not, dear sister, strive not
Is not Jesus the vine and the branch?
Blessed relief!
He is the flower and the leaf
He is the sap, the root and fruit
He is the air and sunshine, soil and showers
Enabling you to grow and bear fruit one hundredfold.

All this is true, so strive not
But continually do His will
Peace and joy and rest is yours
For conscience is tender
Sin instantly seen, confessed and pardoned
Because you rest and strive not.

Let Him dwell in you by faith
This is power and life indeed
Rest in Him by faith
This is power and life increased
Bear fruit using all He sends you.

Blessed be, the God of sun and showers!
Holiness in you has begun
And in you is advancing
Holiness in you is complete
As you claim the promises attached to His name
Eternal springs rise within as you rest, complete in Him.

CLIMBING WITH JESUS

I'm climbing the way with Jesus
As never before
The way is steeper and harder
But You are with me, Lord
The last few steps seem too steep
And I'm filled with fear
Lord, please hold and keep
For I'm breathless with that fear.

Lord, strengthen me in my fear
I've looked all around
I'm terrified I'll fall down
Help me to remember that You are around
The way is too high
The price too hard to pay
Lord, help me on the King's Highway.

Please help me climb the final ascent
I shall never be the same again
I want to reach the top in victory
Where my Lord is waiting in eternity
I shall see Your shining face
With joy, as You say:
My child, here is your place by my side
Come abide with me on higher ground.

I stand in amazement
My fears are all gone
I'm gazing from the top of the mount
Receiving from You, my precious crown
I cast it down at Your feet
Thank You, Lord, for granting victory.

NEW LIFE CREATED

New life created from within
Through the breath of God
Yield to the Hand which moulds
And makes you like Him
Yes, like Christ you shall be
Forever in eternity.

I've started the work
Completion will come and you will be mine again
Through heaven's gardens you shall walk
In fellowship with Father, Spirit and Son
Complete in one
Then hurry, created day
When Jesus shall come to take me home!

WALKING HOME

Hold the nail-scarred Hand
That leads you home
Plant yourself firmly in His side
Wounded and pierced for you.

Walk home in faith
Let your doubts fly
Jesus, your Saviour, is nearby.

Walk home in Victory
Cleaving to the Son
Who died for you and me
Walk home in joy
Walk home in strength
Blessed are you
Who have not seen
Yet believe.

Walk home, spending time with God
Reading His Word
Appropriating His Presence
In all that you do.

Walk home the way of Calvary
Walk home in victory
Holding His Hand
Let Him lead you
Walking to God.

Our Father the Potter
Who moulds us as clay
Remembering those Hands
That are gently moulding
Were nail-pierced that day

Christian, walk home and on to God!

A PACE OF LIFE

The pace at which we live
Is far too quick
Rushing here and there
Not even a moment to spare
To give people a happy smile
To make them happy for a while
Life demands this tremendous pace
I find it hard to keep my place
In this world.

I hate the modern rush
What the world demands of me
And my family and friends
Where will it all end? I don't know
Why do we rush, to and fro?

LOOKING BACK

I look back on my life
And there has been a thread
Continuously weaving and running through
I know, Lord, it is You.

Praise You
For protecting me from harm
Being with me and keeping me calm
How rich and generous You are
Coming so very far
Setting me free from my bondage
Graciously into my life You came
You've opened heaven's door
I cannot ask for anything more.

So help me in return
To give You more of myself
Each passing hour
So that I can shout
Even so, Lord Jesus, come!

EASTER

The Son has risen this morning
He never fails
Bringing life, beauty and glory
But first let me tell you a special story.

There was a man, the only man born to die
He never sinned or told a lie
We took Him and nailed Him to a wooden tree
Where He hung for you and me
To give us liberty and set us free
But we didn't know it then
His special friends
Saw his death to the very end
His agony and pain
Was His to suffer alone
He did this, so you and I could abundantly live.

But my story continues on
Because at the rising of the son
The tomb where He lay His head
The tomb became empty, His body shed
What did everyone say?
Gossip became the order of the day
His disciples told us what they saw
That Jesus arose, and is alive forevermore.

And so, my story continues on
For this is God's only begotten Son
Who rises fresh each morning, in my heart
For He is the bright and morning star
He is the Risen, conquering Son
Who shines and beams on me
For from sin, He's set me free!

Lord, help me live a life dedicated to You
Telling others the simple truth
That God raised Jesus from the dead
And made Him the living head.

God has a plan for each one
Who put their trust in His dear Son
And because you and I do this
God's plan for us will be made known
Because the Son arose and shone.

STANDING FIRM

Stand firm when the billows roll
Stand firm when the going is tough
Stand firm when you feel you've had enough
Hold fast to your anchor, cast in firm, solid rock
Hold fast in life's stormy blast, as the winds take their toll.

Be pliable, bending with the wind
As you feel you will break under the strain
Let the Saviour hold and take all that life is offering you
Say yes, it's tough, but I walk not alone.

Hold His hand and stand firm
When you feel alone
Be grateful for maturity
Enabling you to stand alone.

Stand firm when the billows roll
Stand firm and steady in your soul
He will make the storm still
Or He will take you through
As you stand and rest
Sure in His love for you.

LOVE OF THE FATHER

Thank You for the love of the Father for me
Thank You for Jesus, who came willingly to die for me
Thank You, Holy Spirit, for dwelling in me
Thank You for Your precious Angel guarding me.

My Father, thank You for Your bountiful love
My Jesus, thank You for Your compassion and
understanding
My Holy Spirit, thank You for Your conviction and
comfort
My Angel, thank You for guarding me.

My Father, I praise You for
Individuality shown to me
Great and rich is Your wonderful source
From where all love stems.

My Father, thank You for Your love that never ends
My Father, the love in my heart worships You
For the love poured forth, from Yours.

LAUNCH OUT

Launch out into the deep
Throw your nets out
Be prepared to take the chance
Knowing God is with you
Holding your hand.

Forget past mistakes
Hold the lessons learnt
Tight in your memory
Never let them fade or fall
Because one day you will recall
The failure you became
Then remember, as you called upon the Saviour's name
How He stooped down from above
And pulled you out from darkness into life and love.

A fresh new start and a fresh new vision
With Jesus in your heart, you can envision
The way ahead can become from failure
To a brand-new relation.

Everything is possible with God
So start afresh and you will see
The faithfulness of the guarantee
That Jesus from above
Can cleanse and fill your heart with love.

LET ME BURN MYSELF AWAY

Let me burn myself away
Because of the love You showed to me that day
When Jesus suffered for me
On that wooden tree
Blood and water gushed from His side
Setting me free, in that torrential tide
All my sins were washed away
I want to say, *Hallelujah!*

There is a wonderful story to tell
To save all those on the way to hell
You only have me, Lord
So weak, trembling and lukewarm
Stir the fire in my heart
To be bold and everyone warn
Unless they repent of their sin
Unless they allow Jesus in
To be Lord of their lives
Their souls shall not survive.

Standing before You on Judgement Day
They will not be able with me to say
As I look You boldly in the face
Jesus is my Lord
He has washed my sin away.

Help me shout all around
That a cure for sin has been found
In the death of Jesus Christ
Who once was dead but who now is alive
Please come to Him, I pray
And let Him wash Your sins away.

A WITNESS FOR JESUS

To be Your witness, Lord
To be Your witness!
Boldness returns, stepping out
Speaking to, living on
The cutting edge of Your Spirit.

To be Your witness, Lord
To be Your witness!
A heart full of thanks
To praise and adore
My Lord!

To be Your witness, Lord
To be Your witness!
Shining from my eyes
Knowing in my being
Jesus is alive!

To be Your witness, Lord
To be Your witness!
To save, nourish with growth
Your creation man.

To be Your witness, Lord
To be Your witness!
To abide and love all people
Given to my hand.

To be Your witness, Lord
To be Your witness!
Glorifying Your name
Hastening Your Kingdom
Where all magnify Your name.

All power is available to me, Lord
To be Your witness!
Lord, go before and use, even me!

A FLOWER

A flower, what is it?
An extension of my Father's heart
Each petal is gentle and spread apart
Yet joined in one at the heart
Firm, delicate and fresh
Opening to the Son, radiating colours
Reaching tall and stretching to the sun's rays
As it rises each fresh new day.

A drop of dew, misty on the petal
Glistens and speaks of nature
As she listens to the hearts and needs of all her flowers.

A flower, what is it?
An extension of my Father's heart
A flower in God's hallowed garden
A flower in God's hallowed hand
My Father, so gentle and tender
My Father the Gardener, in life's flower bed.

Peace, joy and stillness are there
In my Father's hallowed garden
My Father, life's Gardener
May I walk this hallowed hour
In the garden of Your care.

MY NAME IS IN HIS HANDS

My name is in His Hands
I am written on the palm of His Hands
Jesus is His name
There is a nail print as a scar
He holds me and I am safe
I'm never too heavy and never too small
Those hands are there each time I fall.

Hold me, Saviour, in Your Hands
For there I long most to be
Wounded and precious Hands
Bleeding for me
Oh, the love of Calvary
Bless You for dying for me.

FAITH

By faith, I praise You, Jesus
That You hold my hand
As we walk to the Promised Land
You take care of me
I am with You in eternity.

By faith, I praise You, Jesus
My life is hid in Christ
That You willingly came
And took my shame
Heaven's door opened to my face
And I saw heavenly grace.

By faith, I praise You, Jesus
For love shed abroad in my heart
That You knew me from the very start
And I am one of the chosen race
And will see You, face to face.

By faith, I praise You, Jesus
That none can pluck me from Your hand
As I pilgrim on
By faith, not by sight or feeling
This is my song.

By faith, I praise You, Jesus
That by faith I abide in You
This life is not the end
Because Jesus is my God and friend
Whose promises are mine.

By faith, I praise You, Jesus
Singing and clapping my hands
Come, Lord, take me to the Promised Land
Where I shall be complete in You
Oh! Jesus, I love You!
By faith, I praise You, Lord!

BEING PLANTED

I must grow where I am planted
That is Your will for me
Many times from my circumstances
I long to be free
At all times in my circumstances
You long to set me free.

I long to grow strong, straight and tall
In my Christian walk, like a sturdy tree
I long to mature in personality, too
Results are not what You want
But the formation of a character
Is Your desire for me.

You never change in Who You are
You didn't carry Your Cross in sin and shame
You used Your Cross to glorify Your Father's name.

Help me to grow, straight and true
Help me grow in my walk with You
I desire to grow where I am planted
Help me, my Father, life's Gardener.

And if You will it and if I need it
According to Your will, You will transplant me.

Until that day, graft me into Your bleeding side
And in that powerful flow of life through my stem
Help me to grow where I am planted
So be it, Lord, and Amen.

SPRINGS IN VALLEYS

Lord, You make springs flow in the valley
Lord, make a spring within me
And from that spring, teach me as I flow in my valley.

Let Your spring swell with the sun's glow
Until a river of life from me flows
In that wonderful flow
Allow me to run where people go.

Help me quench the thirst
Of sinners here below
May life abundant be theirs
As they call upon Your name
May they grow into sturdy trees
As they receive showers of blessing from You.

Make them cheerful with Your oil
Feed them Your bread and increase their strength
As they journey to life's end.

Lord, make a spring flow in my valley
And when I hear Your command
I shall gush to the promised land
To the place prepared for me
Then Your spring shall flow
From Your altar for eternity.

Lord, I can't hold much but I can overflow!
May Your Holy Spirit
Become a fresh spring within me

Amen.

TODAY FOR THAT DAY

To live today for that day
When clouds of heaven part
The day my Redeemer comes
To fully take my heart.

Great and wonderful day
Heaven and earth shall pass away
A new day that's shining forth
A new kingdom of peace
Evil is gone
Hallelujah!

New heaven and earth shall descend
The bride of Jerusalem shall ascend
To live where God is forever to be
A dwelling place for you and me.

I lift my heart in praise
How I long for that day
So, Lord, take my hand today
To live expectantly for that day
A great day and a coronation day!
We throw our crowns towards the throne
At last, we are HOME!

PICKING FRUIT

I would have preferred to pick it
From Galilean shore
But it is only from the local tearoom store
This, though, does not matter
For it's a fruit of priceless treasure
Picked from the very land
That felt the touch of our Saviour's Hand.

So I bring this fruit to you, a gift to eat
And as you taste the sweetness, may it bring a new desire
To walk where Jesus walked along the Galilean shore
Israel, here we come!

A TREE

I trust in Thee and am likened to a tree
I thrust myself to Your life-giving stream
I fear not when the heat of temptation comes
And spiritual dryness casts its spell.

Your promises are mine
I shall flourish and grow under Your life-giving flow
Thank You for Your promise to me that I am like a tree
Planted by the water
Quench my thirsty soul and I shall bear fruit
One hundredfold for You.

TEACHING ME?

Lord, what are You teaching me?
Child, that I am your sufficiency
Come and find your rest
And on my bosom, lay your weary head
Child, come home to me
For above all, I love you.

My child, do you love me?
Oh Lord, in my frail weakness, I come and say yes
Laying my head upon Your breast!
Weary, I find eternal rest
Father God, You know that I love You above all
I come to You and find my rest.

GOD'S CARE

As I go deeper into You
The wonderful truth becomes clear
You come deeper into me
Down into my being
Where no one sees me weep.

You come to touch
Restore, love and heal
You come to bring comfort
Light, joy and release.

Gently Your spirit works Your cause
To lift Jesus higher in my life
Deeper into You and deeper into me.

Child, truth shall set you free
As I do my work in you
This wonderful truth
My child, where you weep
I shall place my feet.

Holy ground shall take the place
Of that empty and barren place
Renewing love is now there.

Child, as you lay your being bare
I shall abide, standing there
Renewing love, faith and hope
My precious child, take courage
For I live to heal and forgive.

I take courage in my Lord
As You work in me
Continue, Lord, to set me free
So that I am ever more devoted to You.

SPRING

Our dark earth is now yielding her fruit
Bulbs bearing flowers are peeping through
First in nature's birth
Is the smallest green shoot
Breaking the hard crust of frost and snow
But nothing can stop this growth!

Flowers so gaily coloured
Pastel and dark hues
All suggest a new season is beginning!

Trees are budding
With a promise of food
For all the birds singing joyfully
And nesting here and there!

Nature once dormant, awakening again
Brings creation a sense of cheer
People are smiling and are happier as days go by
We now know why
For surely, Spring has arrived!

DEATH'S STING

Death, oh death, where is your victory?
Oh grave, where is thy sting?
Through eternal portals
I see heavenly joy waiting for me
The glass may be clouded, but beyond I can see
Jesus, my Lord, shrouded in glory
Waiting there for me (amen)!

Take my life and take my all
You gave Your life and You gave Your all
So that I could join You, beyond death's door
Praising and living with You, forevermore
Praise rises from my soul
As by Your grace
I reach my eternal goal.

PEDESTALS OF PRIDE

I am on a pedestal, a pedestal of pride
Who put me there – did I?

I cannot blame anyone else
I enjoy my pride
I feel exalted and swollen my being
Pride has no right to a place in my life
For eventually, it brings suffering and strife.

Did this not happen to others?
Your word says pride is wrong
So off my pedestal I must come.

Am I willing?
Pride makes me feel good
Am I willing?
To humble myself before You
And confess to the King of Glory
Plead my story that I am full of self
When I profess to be a partaker of divinity.

There is no pride in my God
There shall be no pride in me
So I come on bended knee, and I pray
Lord, help me at the cross
To lay my pride there
Knowing You really care.

Help me not to take my pride back again
Strengthen me, let the truth be seen in me
As I humble myself before Your Son
Be gentle, Lord, as You mould my character
Mentally, emotionally and spiritually
Shape me with Your Potter's Hands
Make me the perfect vessel
For a cracked vessel, I refuse to be
When this vessel of mine is complete
I know You have proved again that You are true.

For on that day, I shall be complete in Your mansion
And in Your mansion, there is a place
For this perfectly moulded vase!
Thank You, Jesus, my all!

PHYSICIAN'S BALM

Deep searing, like a knife stabbing is the hurt
Search out these weeping, sore wounds
That cause so much pain and anguish.

Great Physician, pour out the balm
And comfort You give, and as You do this
Help me learn from these experiences and live
Teach me to pray, have patience and confidence
Help me to trust You each day
Help me bear the burden
And share one day with someone else
The Comfort You have given to me.

And as time passes by
Help me look back and see
The victory and help You've given me.

THE SPIRIT AT WORK

Praise You that my guilt has gone
Forever cast away
But the past has left a scar
My Heavenly Father knows
My wound is not a scratch
My Heavenly Father knows
My wound is deep and tender.

The Holy Spirit will
By the Father's command
With Jesus praying at God's Right Hand
Make the name of Jesus
As ointment poured forth
Upon my wound, so painfully torn.

The Balm of Gilead
By the Physician's skill anoints my sore
Soothes the wound that hurt and pain tore
As He continues day by day, anointing
In His presence I must lay
Continuing with Jesus at the core of my being.

Day by day, the pain will fade away
The wound will heal and I will in faith
Give You praise
Life and Glory, fresh reviving fills my soul
Thank You, Jesus, for making my wound heal and whole.

MEMORIES

Be with me in my memories, Lord
Let the joy override the pain
Of seeing loved ones again
Let Your joy fill my soul
Making me completely whole
Let my face constantly smile
As I hide the pain, for a little while.

Bring me comfort, Lord
I am not asking You to take me round
Above or beneath the pain
Lord, take me straight through the middle of the agony
Help me, so that people will see
Jesus Christ, glorified in me.

PAIN

Lord Jesus, I have pain and hurt in my side
Thank You that the spear pierced Your side
Because the water and blood gushed out
You can identify with me now
Because of the pain You had to bear
You can sympathise with my tears
They fall from unlimited source
Never seeming to end
Thank You that tears ease my pain.

How grateful I am
That You stood the storm around You
For now, Your love surrounds me
I will never have to stand alone
For You call me Your very own
Because the waters poured forth
From Your hurt and pain inside
Healing now springs forth
Like a torrential tide
Taking away the hurt and pain
Never to be remembered again.

You committed Your cause to the Father
For the joy that was set before You
Enabling You to suffer pain
Then the Father took You home again
Seating You at His Right hand.

So please, show me the wonderful plan
That enables me to bring my pain to You
Show me the joy set before me
Jesus, I do believe, help my unbelief in Thee.

JONAH

Put my trust in God
In the depths of the sea
When mighty waves roll over me?
When banished to the gates of hell
Light shining forth, my chains choking me
Put my trust in Thee?

Yes, I will!
For You alone can save me, calming the waves
Bringing light, life and liberty
Is this my reason for praising Thee
In the knowledge You can free me?

In the darkness at the gates of hell
The wonderful story shall be told
That I shall leave all in Your Hands
And at Your word of command
The darkness will no longer cover me
For God does control the billowing seas
In the darkness, I await Thy command
Say the word, then plant my feet on solid ground
I shall then follow You to the place
Where You want me to be!

DEEP AND DIG

Deep and dig into the soil
Work and strive and toil
How hard we've made it, Lord
For it wasn't like this
In the beginning, Lord.

Perfect and good with flowers, trees and fruit
Surrounded us and Your love, too
Then we sinned
The whole of creation turned upside down
Animals fought, killed and died
Adam and Eve began to lie.

We hid away that fateful day
In shame we could not look
At each other and at You
For we knew the truth
We had sinned against You.

Our foolishness and disobedience meant death
For ourselves and all the rest of creation
Forgive us, Lord
For bringing death to all You adore.

SACRED TEAR

His sacred tear splashed from His eye
Child, if you knew the delight
I have prepared
You would look at
The one whom was pierced
Ah, sorrow fills my soul
The wound, torn and raw
Come to me
In your fear
Sacred tear
Splashing from fullness
How long?

Bitter fruit
Drink with dregs
Oh! Bitter cup
Bitter drink
Come not near my lips again
Ah, sacred tear
Trickling down
Cheek and chin
Waterfall of my heart
How long?
Sacred tear
Splashed from His eye
Breaking into a million fragments
Taste
Salt
Weep and shudder
Sacred tear, why fall?

Voice of man, I proclaim
Sacred tear falls to cleanse your shame
Father, anchor my heart to Your heart
Anchor my soul to Your soul
Breath of my breath
Make me whole
Sacred tear, release me.

LOVE

What is this thing called love?
It can be exotic, stimulating thoughts and emotions
Losing control of one's will to another's desire.

What is this thing called love?
It can be painful and hurting with bleeding wounds inside
Caused by losing control of one's will to another's desire.

What is this thing called love
If it is of the flesh, not born of God?
Then the pathway ahead will be bleak, dark and
disturbing
Why? Because we need God
For God is love and he who dwells in God
Dwells in love.

I pray, help me dwell in You
Then the love I have
Will last my whole life through.

IT IS FINISHED

It is finished!
Christ's triumphant cry!
It is finished!
Doubts, faith's shadows fly.

The full and perfect atonement
Satisfaction for my sin
Paid by my Substitute
Who knew no sin.

It is finished!
What is left for me to do?
Only fall on my knees
To praise and worship You.

It is finished!
I praise You forevermore
It is finished!
You have opened heaven's door.

It is finished!
Christ's triumphant cry
It is finished!
Doubts, faith's shadows fly!

GLORY OF THE LORD

Come out, my child, into life and light
Be bound no more by sin and death
I've rolled the stone away, and its consequences too
Light and glory shall shine through!

You shall see
If you believe
Be expectant in your hope
Believe
I will help you in your unbelief.

Our Father listens to My prayers
To prove to you He cares
For your situation
And will meet you in your desperation.

Come out, my child
Into life and light
Bondage and sorrow rolled away.

Enter God's light today
Walk forth from the tomb
Away from darkness and its gloom
I await your obedience
Proof that you believe the Voice of Heaven.

Help waits at the grave's door
Loving hands to set you free
That you may walk in liberty with Me.

Come out, my child, into life and light
Be bound no more
Jesus, take me as I am
I come!

A SONG

The song of Jesus for me
As He was nailed on the tree
At Calvary is as sweet now as then.

I die, He sang, to set her free
That she should fear no more, dying on earth's shore.

I die that in her freedom, she might serve
Living on earth's shore.

I die that she might come home, to everlasting arms
I die, that she might sing
But I live to secure the song that she sings all day long.

I live within the veil
So that she may with boldness come
I live to pray for her
And one day, I'll bring her home
Where she will dwell with Me eternally.

I died, now I live, to sing over her
The sweet song of salvation
For now, she belongs to me
Because of the music played at Calvary.

Thank You, Jesus, for writing the music
And composing the song
That has set me free.

TEACH ME THY WAY

Teach me thy way, my Father, through the pain
Help me restore right relationships again
Take the hurt and take the pain
Teach me thy way, my Father, through the pain
Help me build with the carpenter's love
A heart and a home for You, filled with love.

And as I look to You above
Remembering Your banner over me is love
Teach me thy way, my Father, through the pain
Help me never to cause lament or pain
Building my heart out of the Solid Rock
With You, cleansing the hurt
And always looking and taking stock.

Oh! Master Builder, take my heart of stone
And fill with it Your love
Change it and restore and heal
Overflowing my heart's reservoir
To love all forevermore.

And Father, when the hurt is in control
Lead me gently home to Your heart
Filled with love for me
Where in Your heart
There is eternal love and rest for me.

Rested and restored I shall become
Abiding in the Great I Am
Hold me close as I open my heart's door
To step out and live once more
Teach me thy way, my Father.

CARING

You looked tired today
Tenderness crept forth from me
I desired to comfort you
To wrap my arms around you
I longed to hold you close.

Tenderness continued flowing from me
I longed to comfort and to share
To hold, cherish and to care.

I wonder if the tension would have eased from your eyes
Would your restlessness have ebbed like a tide?
Would you have inwardly become calm
As I held you in my arms?

I wanted to comfort you until the storm inside you
became still
I longed to see pleasure appear in your eyes
I longed to have you relax by my side
I wonder if I could have done all this for you
I wonder if I dare to reach out to you.

Our friendship, fragile as a butterfly, may have changed
So forgive me, for I was scared to lose all we've already
shared
Was it worth the chance to reach out and hold your
hand?
I'll never know, will I? For, my friend, I let you go.

NARROW WAY

The way is narrow and difficult
But never claustrophobic
Jesus is my shining light
I need not be filled with fear
For on the path, He is near.

Jesus holds me all the way
He leads and guides and I must trust
For it is for my eternal good.

Lord, I do get frightened on Your way
Hold me close and then I can feel
Your loving embrace.

Which shall I choose, the broad, wide path into death?
Or the narrow way with Jesus into life?
Day by day, I have to make the choice
Am I a coward, or with Jesus shall I rejoice?

I choose the narrow path to life
With Jesus by me, as my guide.

STANDING ON HOLY GROUND

I stand on Holy Ground
With fire all around
How awesome is the sight
Of God's flame, burning bright
He consumes that which in me
Needs to be set free
My sandals off, I stand, then kneel
At this terrible liberty
Communion of hearts take place
And as I hear God's voice
Wonders never cease to be
God, eternally, loves me.

This marvellous love is shared
As two hearts blend into one
I have now become
Like Jesus, His precious Son
This truth now sets me free
To walk in service with You
I rise, quickened by Your grace
Gazing into Your wondrous Face
Light reflects and shines on me
Oh, glorious liberty!

Looking into the face of God
I see myself, son of sod
Burnt to ashes, all myself
That which remains is purity.

I rise, quickened by Your Spirit
Shoes on, to spread the good news
Down into valley and vale
Come everyone, His blood avails
To make clean and to share
His eternal life, beyond compare.

ALWAYS SEEING AND ALWAYS CARING

Always seeing
Always caring
Always loving me!
Always there
Always allowing me
To be free!
Always sharing my life
Bringing me through strife
Always wanting to give me the best
As, in Him, I rest.

On life's journey I am bound
Walking with God, no matter what
He keeps me safe and sound
How I love You, my Lord
Strengthen me through Your Word
I know Jesus is mine
Right into eternity's time.

Let me pass the message to you
That Jesus, our Lord, will see you through
Truly, Jesus is mine
Live for Him too
And your life will shine.

FRIENDSHIP

Shall I give you my all
So you stand proud, straight and tall?

Shall I share my character, too
Enabling you to grow?

Shall I give you my all
Not with thought of receiving in turn?

Shall I give you my all
To comfort, love and support you?

My all I give, take and let us live
Separate, yet for each other.

May I give you my all?
The answer lies with you
My friend, I shall be true
In friendship with you!
Is your answer ready?
Will you reach out
And accept what I'm giving?

Reach out, my friend, say *Yes!*
Smile and let us live separate
Yet for each other!
I await your answer
May I be that friend for you?

FEELING ALONE

I stand alone, deserted by all that I love
Hurt, despondent and judged
By all those saved by Your Blood.

Anger, hurt and bitterness
Rage within my soul
Hurt them, but make me whole
Oh Lord, how selfish I've become.

I feel incomplete and I suffer
Needing their warmth and love
I'm still rejected
By those saved by Your Blood.

I pray, commune and in peace
Remember that God is my friend
Who stood completely alone.

My friend, God, take my hurt
Fellowship with me, to life's end
I must forgive - can I?
No, yet my Saviour says Yes, it must be so.

Me, to forgive and forget
To cherish them without neglect?
Will this strife never end?
I'm judged by You, my brother
With no one to defend, except
You, my God and Friend.

Thank You, Lord, for those precious few
Who have seen me through
Though alone I still stand.

I rest my case with You
I rest my judgement in Your Hands
Guilty is still their awesome shout
I cry but rest, complete in You.

THE TEARS

Once more, the tears are here
I question and doubt, cry and fear
I know You will use these for my good
Because of this, I express to You my love
As I lay my soul bare.

I know the truth of Your word
Lord Jesus Christ, thank You
You have died for me, nailed onto a tree
Cursed You became in God's sight
So that with Him I would be set right
Now from sin I am set free
Pardoned, cleansed and at liberty.

Help me remember, freedom is not a license to sin
But the grace to come back in
To say that I'm sorry
And then Your arms fold me gently in
And in Your tender mercy and grace
I know for me there is peace.
Amen!

HAPPY TODAY

I was so happy to hear your voice today
Love had me on its swing
As my heart danced and swayed.

You do wonderful things for me
I hear your voice and I want to cry
Thank you that you have noticed I am alive!

The very vibrancy of my being
Tinkles with laughter, because of you!
I want to love you
And bring happiness to you.

Love will then have you on its swing
And your heart shall dance and sway
For I intend to do
Wonderful things for me and you!

A BIRTH JOURNEY

It's very dark
Claustrophobic
I make no movement
There is no sound
And there's no light
It's strange.

Hearts are pounding
Touch is hurting
Turbulence and distress
I'm moving now
Flowing waters
It's strange.

I sense a change
New sights as I stretch
This way up, then down
Security
Strength and content
It's strange.

Feeling large and light
I seek, looking
Then I see two faces
My beloved
It's very good
It's strange.

New life and peace
For you and me
In love, I'm born alive
Yet born again
My cry is heard
It's strange.

Take care of us
Your precious family
Enjoy, nourish and
Guard with prayer
And then, with praise
Thank God!

AM I NOT A CHRISTIAN?

Many people tell me that I am not a Christian
They point a finger at all I do
And say I can't belong to You.

Do I believe them? People like me, sinners?
Whose word I cannot trust?
Or do I believe God, whose word I can trust?
I opened my life to You
You promised to come in
And You came in, Amen!

I thank and praise You, Father
I believe and trust in Your word and Your promises!
And Lord, those times that I let You down
And gossip gets around
Help me to remember
You can take care of Your name
For I know that I will never be the same
Your love draws me back again.

I have the victory in You
For there is no blame
Attached to my name
For You, dear Lord, hung in shame
On that terrible, yet wonderful day
When You bore my sins away!

WE SING

We sing, come into my heart, Lord Jesus
Yet we say, but only in part
You can have all of me
Yet not that dark little part
I've closed the door and lost the key
You say, my child, I have the master key.

Jesus, I don't want You in my heart's dark place
For if You open that door, in flows amazing grace
The darkness there will be flooded with Your light
All my secrets that I can no longer hide
What a precious price to pay
Yet the darkness will be washed away.

I fear but I know
This is healing for my soul
For Your light brings release
Comfort, joy and increase
So use Your master key
My Lord, You can have that part of me.

Your Spirit's work is for my good
Too long, my ground I have stood
I'm willing for Your ever searching grace
To deal with my heart's dark place
Take, now, Your master key
My Lord, have Your own sweet way with me!

HEART OF THE FATHER

Out of the heart of the Father
Came the pure, sweet and white dove
Out of the heart of the Father
Sent with pure, sweet love
Torrential love poured forth
To claim my heart forevermore.

I am created to bring You pleasure
I am called to serve You
God of all gods
King of all Kings
Sweet and precious dove.

Thank You for what You have done for me
Thank You for salvation, full and free
Eternal purposes are in store
As l live in You and praise You forevermore.

Out of the heart of the Father
Came the pure, sweet and white dove
Resting on me eternally
May the joy from You
Be seen in this dark world
Help all to understand
You are waiting in the promised land
Jesus praying there, at Your right hand.

Out of the heart of the Father
Came the pure, sweet and white dove
Sent in pure and righteous love
To live, abide and indwell
To strengthen, comfort and help
Praise You, Father and Son
And comforting Sweet Dove.

A FRIEND'S WEDDING

The wedding bells are chiming
Eyes are shining
Love is being
The wife is glowing
Forever entwined
To her husband who is Thine.

Bless them together, Lord
Help them work for You
Strengthen and bind the two
So that they will be
A blessing together for You!

JEALOUSY

What are these feelings invoked in me
I recognise them as jealousy
They are soul destroying, hurtful and painful
They try to destroy my love and trust
They search every corner of my heart bare
Causing pain and anxiety everywhere.

Fight them, I must
Help me, Lord
To love and trust You to the very end
I will destroy the jealousy
Before the jealousy destroys me.

I will not give in to hurt and pain
I will trust in Your love for me again
Continue the fight, I must do
For our love will win through
By God's tender mercy and grace
As daily together, we seek His face.

THE SANDS OF TIME

The sands of time glisten in the sun
Warm and running through fingers
That touch and linger on the edge of the sea.

How long have you been there?
Sands of our time, stories to tell
Yet never written in a book
On the edge of eternity
Sands of Time.

I WANT TO BE FREE TO BE ME

I want to be free to be me
I know You, Lord, love me
Thank You.

Will You set me free to be me
Yet committed fully to You?
I fight and struggle with self
Help set me free and I will be
Forever praising Thee.

THREE PRECIOUS FRIENDS

I have three friends, Helen, Judy and Joan
Who like to have a good groan and moan!
They chatter like birds, ten to a dozen
And forget the cakes, burning in the oven
One is fair and one is dark
The other plays the piano and sings like a lark
Joan is the one who is always late
Helen lives her life on a pair of skates
Judy - yes, well, the secrets one could tell!

I promise if you meet these three
They'll always offer you a cup of tea
But watch out, for up their sleeve
They have tricks galore that make you roar
When you see them in our town
You will always know they are around
Just listen for giggles, laughter and fun
And together they weigh nearly a ton!
Helen likes a spotless kitchen floor
So please remember to wipe your feet at the back door.

I miss being in Helen's kitchen corner
Sat on my stool like little Jack Horner
I miss the dishes in Judy's sink
If wishes came true, I'd dry them all again!
I miss my sandwiches at lunchtime with Joan
For I also miss having a good groan and moan!

If you see these three friends of mine
Tell them in my heart they'll always shine
For they are very special to me
May the Lord bless them now, and eternally!
Girls, you will never know
How I miss all of you so
Praise the Lord, for together we will be
Friends and sisters in Christ, eternally.

PRAYER AND TRUST

In no better hands, Lord
Can I place my precious friend
Than Yours, that circle and never end
Wide, deep and abundant is Your love
And in Your care above
I place the one I'm praying for
And whom I dearly love.

All the storms that beset her
Beat and pound her
Will leave their scar
She may feel that Your presence from her is far
But You have promised to make the storm still
And inside her, the emotions shall calm
She will feel Your perfect peace
As she rests in Your everlasting arms.

You will bring her through
As she rests and trusts in You
You know the way she takes
As she lingers in Your sweet embrace
And when You have tried her
She shall come forth as gold
May Your name be magnified
As the story is told
How You took her through the storm
And brought her safely home.

THE SABBATH

Remember the Sabbath
Rejoice, for it is the day God rested
Knowing His completed work was good.

In the same way, Calvary brought about
The finished work of redemption
Jesus sat down and resting, He knew
His completed work was good.

This day of rest is freely given
Remember to rest and rejoice in the day
That the Lord completed
What He had begun, life anew!

ASPECTS OF AUTUMN

I am a leaf on an autumn tree
The season of life is changing me
I turn from green to gold, then brown
Tinged with red and orange hue
The wind blows on me
Quivering, I lose my grip on all I have known.

I fall safely to the earth
Gentle hands guide my journey
I lay amongst other leaves
Horse chestnuts, acorns and berries rest there too
Near mother earth's roots.

Feet now are treading the ground
Making a crunchy sound
Little hands take the fruit of this season's birth
And I feel alone, my purpose denied.

The wind strongly blows me against my will
I dance with delight
I am swirled, tossed and twirled
It is good to be part of the sky again
If only for a little while.

I lay quiet again
Days pass and I'm slowly drying
Then it's wet and I feel I'm dying
I'm blending with the moist earth
I now realise this is my second birth
I am a leaf and still part of nature's plan
I am finding that I am one with the tree
That gave birth to me.

She is branch, trunk and root
She is bud, leaf, flower and fruit!
How clever autumn is
Through nature's design
I and the tree are both still alive!

SET FIRM

I have set you firmly in your foundation of solid rock
You shall never be moved
I have placed my Son's blood
Over your wilful failures in sin
And I see His shed blood, cleansing you
You shall never be moved.

Mountains and valleys are all the same to me
I, your Lord, control the circumstances in your life
You shall not be moved.

I rebuke Satan and problems in your life
You shall be free
Otherwise, in my wisdom for your growth
They shall remain, trust me.

So far and no further is my command
To the distressing and billowing seas
That overwhelm and condemn, so trust me.

You will never be so submerged again
By those rising seas that your spirit be broken
Trust me, for when I say it is enough
My child, you shall never be moved.

TIMES OF NEED

Oh, I thirst for my God
Rain showers of love upon me
Let my heart tender become
As I turn to Your Son.

Plant seeds there
That bring life and sweetness
Out of life's barrenness
Father, let my heart melt away
And in its place
Plant Your love for all to see
Let it be true
As I rest in You
Flowers bloom and fruit increasing
As I turn my face towards You.

I rise, quickened by Your Spirit
My feet travel home
To Your tender Heart
A place for me
Thanks to Calvary.

Oh, Lamb of God, come soon
Take me home
Where I shall dwell
With You eternally!

JIMMY!

I know a guy called Jimmy
Who is tall and rather skinny!
He has peace and joy in his eyes
Reminding me God is alive.

He thinks, laughs and plays
Enjoying life in every way
Sometimes he gets into a state
Pressures piling up, day by day
He takes them all in his stride
Confident and assured the Lord is by his side.

He really has helped me a lot
I'm grateful for his ministry
Talking with him has led me through
To a more precious relationship with You
I hand him over to You
And ask that You keep him close to You.

This is my prayer
Love, bless and keep him
Do all this for me, starting now
And finishing in eternity
In the name of Jesus, I pray.

A LARK IS ON THE WING

The lark is on the wing as I remember you
The sun stands still as I think of you
The stars shed their tears
And the moon loses its shine
Because you are no longer mine.

Time passes by
The field mouse gently lies in the meadow
And the lark is still on the wing.

Darling, were you a dream or
One day, will we fly?
Above the mountains, majestic, high.

Above tall, green trees
Darling, come fly with me?
Let us leave the world
Let the stars cry with joy
Moonbeams shine
As the sun rolls around the world
And we are together again.

Yes, the lark is on the wing
But one wing is leaning in the wind
For I know the truth
I cannot fly, for you are no longer mine.

The lark still flies on the one wing
And I shall be the same without you
For, my darling, the other wing is you!

GAZE UPON HIM

Gaze upon Him
Whose beauty lies within the veil
Free for all to see
Who come by His grace.

Jesus, by faith
I look upon Your Face
May I see such beauty there
That will keep me sitting there.

Reflect Yourself upon my soul
May others see upon my face
The glory of Your love and grace
Jesus.

A BABE IS BORN

A babe is born
Proclaims the star
Angelic throngs sing out
Blessed is Bethlehem
We too are blessed
Jesus, Son of Righteousness
Has come to take our sins away
The only babe born to die
The future is set
King of all mankind
Is born tonight.

Let hallelujahs ring out
Hope for all mankind
Is born in stable bare
So bring your praises to the King
Shout Hosannah!
Lift your hands in delight
The Saviour of the world
Is born tonight!
Hallelujah!

HEART'S DESIRE

Fill me with Your Glory, Lord
So in my heart, You are adored
Forever and forever, I will be
Praising Jesus living in me.

Each step I go onward bound
Jesus is there and I'm safe and sound
What can I say?
Except Praise to my Father on the throne
Shall come from my lips, for He's made me His own.

Praise and lifting up my soul
To God, who has made me well and whole!

TRUE FRIENDS

True friends, how dear they are
For they help to heal wounds that are raw
They give love and understanding
Of themselves without demanding
How can we live without good friends
To see us through to the end?

I pray the Lord will let me be
Worthy of them, and be faithful to see
When they are in hurt and pain
Then I can give back what I've gained.

NEW THINGS

Child
I am doing a new thing
Do you not perceive it?
Child
It is now springing forth
Reaping eternal joy
From me for you
For us
Together.

Child
Remember not or cling to
Suffering, strife and stagnant life
I do not, so then
Listen to my command
With a promise.

Child
Do you perceive
That which I intend to do?
Eternal springs
Shall rise within
To quench
Your thirsty soul.

Child
I will give you life
And I will be faithful
To that life
I only ask one thing
In this life I'm giving to you
Praise and serve me
Letting my Love
Fill your soul
My precious child
I am devoted to you!

HEART AND SOUL

My heart and soul are filled with tears
Rising, choking and swelling
When it will end, there is no telling
The misery and pressure, Lord
Is so hard to bear, help me share
These feelings with You.

Gently, use the Balm of Gilead
As I express to You
The hurt within my soul
Cleanse me and make me whole.

To Your Glory, Lord
For as I slowly heal
Learning to trust You each day
People will say:
How does she have the victory in her life
As she struggles with bitterness and strife?
Is her God real? Can I trust Him too?

My prayer is for them that they will realise
That our God is real, and they can trust Him too
For Jesus does love me and you.

TRUST ME

Trust me for the increase, my child
Trust me, I have all power to avail for you
I care and I know, I will hold and lead
You cannot walk the path of faith
Without my power and saving grace.

Too long you have struggled hard
Release me now, your Lord
My spirit is in control
Be not fearful to let go
I will then work through you
Doing all the things you want me to
My child, trust Me.

JESUS, I FEEL ALONE

Jesus, I feel alone
My child, I was alone.

Jesus, I feel rejected
My child, I was rejected.

Jesus, no one understands
My child, no, not like I can.

My child, open your heart
Let me cleanse the void
Your need I'll meet
From my word.

Jesus, I open my heart
Joyfully to You
My precious Jesus
I'm reaching out to You.

My child, remember
What I've done for you
I dearly love you
My child, you have received
Help on the narrow way.

Love and tenderness are yours
From unlimited source
Call upon my name
I'll touch you with the Living Flame.

My child, I had to walk alone
I am by your side
Every day and every night
Cast all care upon me
Keep your eyes on my face
Keep your hand firm in mine
We're together in eternity's time.

My child, you've received my Spirit
Let him reign
Release Him to take control
Remember, you'll never walk alone.

Walk on with hope in your heart
Walk on with faith and hope in Me
Walk on through eternity
My child, remember, you have never had to walk alone.

Thank You, Jesus, for walking alone for me.

LAUGHTER

God will give me laughter in days that lie ahead
For He will do what was promised
Through the Living Head.

Jesus is the promised Son
And as I journey on
Belief will spring from joy unseen
As I see what God's prepared for me.

Then laughter from my heart
Will flow like mountain streams
To God be the glory
For He will keep His word to me!

This fulfilled in precious time
Will be His blessing to me
Laughter from the wells of God
Fulfilled Word shall make me whole!

DARK AND BLEAK

Dark and bleak is the way to hell
Lonely, fearful and unknown
You tread the path along
Falling, crying with despair.

Over Christ's body you have trod
And pushed His face into the sod
He wants to save you from your sin
But you won't let Him in
So tread your path alone
Remember, you have chosen to travel that way
You will be sorry one day.

Because you will on bended knee bow
Before the King of Glory now
Then as you confess, Jesus is Lord
That by His people He is adored
You will then depart from Him
He who, many times, has called you gently in.

Where will you go, to a place without God?
Where no joy, light and peace dwell there
All is dark, torment and bare
And as the tormenting bleakness sets in
Forever, you will be lost in your sin
Remember, you chose hell.

AT THE FEET OF JESUS

Laying all at the feet of Jesus
As never before
Laying all at the foot of the cross
From my willing heart's door
I want to be free from self
I want what You desire for me
I want to be set free
Yet wear the yoke of Calvary.

I want to be free from pain
Yet I want to feel Your pain
The pain You suffer over Your children
As You look upon our situations
I want the bondage of the cross
I want to help others bear their cross
I want to suffer with them for You
I want to glorify and satisfy You
I want to identify, my Lord, with You.

My child, are you willing to endure?
My child, are you quite sure?
Do you know the weight and pain of my yoke?
Do you think the knowledge of Me
And the knowledge of Calvary
Is an easy path to tread?
My child, do you really see the life ahead with me
Has a tremendous responsibility?

There is pain, heartache and sorrow
There will be no easy tomorrow
If you are willing to follow me
You will shed many tears
And go through many times of fear.

My children do need comfort
Go and comfort them for me
This is the work that I prepared for you in eternity
The choice is yours
Answer Me, your Lord.

My Lord, here am I, send me
Then take the fullness of my love
Go, my child, walking in that full and free love
Break the bread and share, tell how I love and care
Keep close to me and talk often with me.

Love, share and know Me
I will then strengthen you
In the work I've prepared for you
All power is available from heaven
Go in my love
With my blessings, my child, go.

ASHES

Come out of the ashes, my child
They are a remnant of fires long ago
A new fire waits to blaze you with life
So let the charred remains go.

Come from that dusty place
To the new one by appointed grace
Let my love light your soul
Come, my child, and be made whole!

THE REDEEMED OF THE LORD

We, the redeemed of the Lord shall return
With everlasting joy upon our heads
We follow the King
Armed with His strength
For He is our shield and refuge
He will part the seas for us
As we onward go with joy and gladness
With praise and worship, we sing.

He is our Redeemer
The Lord of Hosts is His name.

As we awake to God's cry
Clothed in our garments white
We march on to Jerusalem
The marriage feast of our King
With praise and worship, we sing.

He is our Redeemer
The Lord of Hosts is His name.

He redeemed us from our sin
He calls us His very own
Faith arises in our hearts
As we sing His glorious name
With praise and worship, we sing.

He is our Redeemer.

CAST ALL SELF OUT

Cast all self out and let all Jesus in!
Release and let our Lord
Fulfil from His word
Abide and rest with trust and hope
Fear and doubt, we can let these go.

Unending love and help are ours
From the only infinite source
Hold and love, bearing all
Trusting God at His word.

Cast all self out and let all Jesus in
Healing streams will spring within
My dear friend, let go
He also this path trod
He knows, as He suffered too
Three times He prayed
To gain victory for me and you.

Agony poured forth from His physical frame
He totally depended on God's reliable name
He cried, not my will, but thine be done
Casting out self and letting God in.

He totally conformed to the cross
Barriers were cast and thrown away
He lay naked on a tree
For you, dear Christian, and for me.

He took all sin and shame
That was debited to our names
He arose, the resurrected life
He arose, to give us a new life.

He arose, to pray for us each day
Victory is ours
When we whisper His name, Jesus.

Then let us whisper His name, my friends
Casting all self out and letting all Jesus in.

Our lives will never be the same again
Healing will rise within our souls
My friends, let us love and live for Him
Dying to self every day
Jesus is with us every day
Hold tight, my friends
God's power never ends.

Our lives will never be the same again
He can and will do all this for us
If we cast all self out and let all Jesus in!

OUR BABY

The Robin sang merrily in his tree
Then came to visit our family
He flew back and sang:
This baby's a beautiful little thing.

The Bambi came, rabbits, and all their friends too
Looking at the lovely sight
Of baby in the morning light.

Master and King, Lord of everything
Many things are not understood, as yet.

But thank You, Father, giver of all good things
For blessing us with our son
A trophy of Your grace and a child of the King.

TAKE COURAGE IN THE LORD

Take courage in the Lord
Read, meditate on His Word
Take courage in the Lord
Fight Satan with our Sword
Do not listen to his lies
Or take discouragement in those lies.

But take courage in the Lord
Applying His Word
Fighting on to victory
Then the gates of hell
Cannot prevail
Against you, or me
When we are abiding in
The authority
And dynamics of our Lord.

Take courage in the Lord
Claim His name
Knowing He is watching
Over you and me
To keep us safe
So take courage in the Lord
Reading, meditating on His Word.

BE STILL

I am confused
BE STILL
My brain is in turmoil
BE STILL
My thoughts race, flashing by others
BE STILL
They are entwined together, causing fear
BE STILL.

I need to break the triangle of thoughts
BE STILL
I need your words to permeate my being
BE STILL
Your words shall break the triangle
BE STILL
My thoughts shall turn away from self
BE STILL.

My thoughts shall be renewed by You
BE STILL
As I follow Your command to
BE STILL
I shall, by Your grace
Be still and in the stillness, I will give you praise.

FORGIVENESS

Saviour Jesus, what You made beautiful
I desecrated, oh, cleanse and forgive
Lord, please come in
Lord, as You come in
I give myself to You.

Freely take back what is Yours
I worship You
Oh! Lord, in days to come
My eyes will watch and yearn for You
Seeking ever the blessed day
That I will see You, my Lord, face to face
Hallelujah, Lord come!
Even so, Lord Jesus come!

LEAVING FRIENDS

I've had to leave my friends, Lord
We've moved home and town
And though I've settled down
I miss having my friends around
Those few years we were together
Caring and hurting, laughing and crying
Being one and sharing with You
Loving and growing in You
Lord, I miss them, do You understand?

My child, I do understand
As no other can
I shared with my friends, too
I laughed and cried and grew
Loving them enough
To die for each precious one
Then I parted from them in a different way
I became Lord, Master and God
And my relationships changed.

But be not sad
For we shall all be together again
Think of the joy in store
As eternity we all share
Never to be parted again
My plan I have made known
I'm making a mansion and a home
For all our precious friends
Where time never parts or ends.

The scars may remain
We'll never be the same
But He has promised to be with us, each new day
Giving fresh and victorious strength
To overcome once again
As He touches our lives
We will never be the same again
Amen.

HOW CAN I BEAR THE ANGUISH?

How can I bear the anguish?
I feel You have let me down
Yes, my Lord, I blame You
For the state I'm in - why?

I claimed Your promise to me
For now and eternity
Something went wrong, so I doubt and fear You
I am angry with You
But deep inside, I know it was me
I, the middle of sin
Self-stepped in and took control
And everything went out of control.

Lord Jesus, forgive me
Reveal Your greatness to me
Cleanse me, take control
I give You the right once again
To be my Lord, Master and God
Let me see things in eternal light
Seeking the depth of life
Doing things good and right
Only by Your mighty power can I do this
As I seek to learn and live.

A MISCARRIAGE

The Lord cares for thee
He has a wonderful plan
That He will make known
He wants you to belong to Him alone
He knows the suffering you are going through
And He will Love and strengthen you.

His promises to you are true
They are in His Word
Read them and you will become calm
Remember, God knows how you feel
For He also let His Son leave
His presence for 33 years.

Then God took His Son back home again
Your baby is tucked away safe
In God's warm and Loving embrace
Trust, believe, and you will receive Peace.

ONE DAY

One day, will you be yourself with me
And will you really talk with me?
Will you take your mask of indifference off?
Will you tell me what is going on inside you?

One day, will you commune with me?
Letting go and being yourself
So that I can reach and touch
Your hidden beauty inside
I long for that, a tenderness shared
I wish you dared to let me inside your heart.

One day, will you come with me
By the flowers and trees?
Will you share this beauty with me
And in each other, be free?

As a bud opens forth in beauty
Why can't you be the same with me?
Would you; could you?

One day, as we walk along
In quietness as birds sing their song
Will we then get along?
As I reach out and hold your hand
I wonder if you will understand
The gentleness of your hand in mine
Stops the monotony of time
I feel for you.

One day, as love springs forth
Can I then become part of you
If that is not already true?
Partially mine and partially yours
Your love, all mine
If our hearts ever entwine?
That day, let's really talk and really walk
That day in future time, when you may be mine
To share for just a day in time
One day, that day?

DOUBTING AND TRUSTING

Cold and numb, these feelings are new to me
How do I handle them, Lord?
They are attacking me constantly
I cannot stand against the pressure
Give to me, of Your Comfort, a good measure.

These feelings are foreign to my being
How clever Satan is, always seeing
My weak and raw, aching wound.

Satan lies and deceives, whispering in my ears
I believe the lies, and down flow the tears
Then the numbness sets in
For I pay the consequence of my sin.

Lord Jesus Christ, set me free
Hold me tight and give me liberty
Fill me with Your Spirit
So the wound no longer pains
Then I won't ever doubt You again.

Doubt You again?
Yes, I'm sure that I will
But only until
I see Thee face to face
Then glorious will be my praise.

FAMILY

Love is fresh, spring and vernal
God is love, light and eternal
Love is beautiful and glowing
God is never ending and flowing.

Joined together in one
Husband and wife, daughter and son
In Christ, shall forever be
The perfectly moulded family.

MYSTERIOUS STRANGER

The Mysterious Stranger, what did He do?
He endured suffering, rightfully mine
He endured pain at the crossroads of time
He was wounded for me, pierced on the tree
Bruised at Calvary.

The Mysterious Stranger, why did He do it?
His Father willed it and He desired it
Showing me His great love
I was a sheep and lost from the fold
I was missing and going astray
But the Tender Shepherd of old
In that love He sought and then He bought me.

I was lost in sin but His love marched in
I am bought and not my own
I am bought and His alone!
He paid the price on Calvary's tree
By His grace, I live righteously.

The Mysterious Stranger, who is He?
The fairest in the land
Jesus is His wonderful name
No other name shall my heart claim.

A Mysterious Stranger, now no longer to me
My Lord and Master for eternity!
The King Divine, I now serve and I now follow
The Mysterious Stranger is now my best friend
As together we journey to life's end.

SHORT POEMS AND EXPRESSIONS

To have a meal with Jesus
Is fellowship divine
To sit, eat and sup
Living Bread and New Wine
Fill me, Lord, from Your Table
Quench my thirsty soul
And while I'm leaning at Your Table
Make me whole.

Touch me and make me ablaze
Living Torch and Living Flame

Consume me for the coming day
Wonderful day
Jesus is coming again!

Lord, I don't want to be seen as narrow and good
I want to be seen as someone who is free
Yet bound in our Saviour's love!

I long to believe without doubt
I long to trust without fear
Help me, Lord, in my unbelief
Reach out Your hand to me
As You reached out to Peter, on the sea
Lord, save me from unbelief.

Help me to trust You
As You test me
For Omnipotence knows why
And when I fail to trust You
Forgive me, I worship You.

Pray and believe
Trust and obey
And go God's way!

The pleasant green of the hills
Remind me of Your gracious Hand
Caring for me above with total and complete love
Wrapped in His arms, I know and believe and feel
Complete joy and peace, resting in His love.

Watch and pray
Keep temptation at bay!

Be a busy bee
Making cups of tea
With the blue cup and saucer
And you will 'be' what God wants you to be
A very busy bee!

IN GOD'S EVERLASTING ARMS

(Written for Carol Pigford by Colleen Smith, 1983)

My heart feels as if it's breaking
As I think of you in pain
Such a pain, no mortal can understand
For the loss of a son, only God can know and feel
So reach up and let your Daddy (Abba) take your hand.

Open up the floodgates of your tears
You cry for all the mothers through the years
But to have lost a son so very dear
I have to question, WHY?

Oh! Why, Father, should You let this be?
The Father looks down in His Sovereignty
He reaches out His everlasting arms
He wraps you tightly to His chest and rocks you
To the rhythm of the gently swaying palms.

Oh, little daughter who I love
The Good Shepherd is watching His sheep
Neil is one of my special little lambs
So weep, my loved one, weep.

Then save up all your memories
To be taken out and cherished, one by one
But your boy is safe with Me
No more sorrow will Neil see
For He is safe
In the arms of Mary's precious Son.

Printed in Great Britain
by Amazon